Mystics in Spite of Themselves

Mystics in Spite of Themselves

FOUR SAINTS
AND THE WORLDS
THEY DIDN'T LEAVE

R. A. Herrera

William B. Eerdmans Publishing Company

Grand Rapids, Michigan / Cambridge, U.K.

Published 2010 by
Wm. B. Eerdmans Publishing Co.
2140 Oak Industrial Drive N.E., Grand Rapids, Michigan 49505 /
P.O. Box 163, Cambridge CB3 9PU U.K.

Printed in the United States of America

14 13 12 11 10   7 6 5 4 3 2 1

Library of Congress Cataloging-in-Publication Data

Herrera, Robert A.
Mystics in spite of themselves: four saints and the worlds
they didn't leave / R. A. Herrera.
p.   cm.
ISBN 978-0-8028-4861-1 (pbk.: alk. paper)
1. Christian saints. 2. Mysticism.   I. Title.

BR1710.H47   2010

248.2′20922 — dc22
[B]

2009042574

www.eerdmans.com

Contents

Prologue

T HIS brief study attempts to show that active, politi-
cally engaged, religious men, separated by chance or
circumstance from the solitary cell, hermitage, or desert
that was their normal habitat, were nevertheless able to
scale the heights of spirituality, and that they did so during periods of crisis. Having survived the twentieth century, contemporary man is all too familiar with crises, of
which there have been a great number and variety. He is
above all interested in the upset birthed by the nineteenth century, which found its métier in the twentieth.

About a century ago, Max Nordau in *Entartung* (*De-
generation*, 1895) spoke of the *fin-de-siècle* state of mind
characterized by "emancipation from traditional discipline, unbridled lewdness, the unchaining of the beast in
man . . . the end of the established order."[1] A few decades
prior, Baudelaire published sections of a projected work

---

1. Cited in B. G. Brander, *Staring into Chaos: Explorations into the
Decline of Civilizations* (Dallas: Spence Publishing, 1998), p. 23, n. 9.

that was to be called *The End of the World* under the heading of *Fusées* (the flares that ships use to signal emergency), predicting that this world is drawing to a close: "We shall perish by the very thing we fancy that we love. Technology will Americanize us, progress will starve our spirituality . . . universal ruin will manifest itself . . . above all, in the baseness of hearts."[2] The gigantic figure of Nietzsche must also be mentioned. In the last chapter of *Ecce Homo,* written immediately prior to his final collapse in 1889, he announced the advent of a colossal crisis of never-before-seen proportions.[3]

Not every crisis marks a downward turn. There are periods of reassessment and recuperation. What they have in common: at their center, a maelstrom, the void, the lack of fixity and stability; at their periphery, either chaos or a new world. These are not the times of tranquility and order usually required by the religious life for souls to ascend to an elevated state of spirituality. Still, some manage the ascent. The lives and careers of Augustine, Gregory the Great, Anselm of Canterbury, and Ramon Llull are prime examples of this phenomenon.

2. Cited in Brander, *Staring into Chaos,* p. 26.

3. Friedrich Nietzsche, *Ecce Homo.* This is one of the works published by Nietzsche's executors. For complete bibliographic information, refer to Musarian Ausgabe (23 vols., 1920-1929). Perhaps the view essayed in *Ecce Homo* derived from Nietzsche's fear that Darwinian views might undermine the Western tradition of human dignity with dire consequences.

Chapter 1

Introduction

A<small>T FIRST</small> viewing, mysticism appears as something rather vague and amorphous, an umbrella for all types of exotica and erotica. Though personal, cultural, and universal factors are interwoven into these spiritual experiences, the privileged habitat of mysticism remains with the individual, the hermit roasting under the Egyptian sun as contrasted with the army of frenzied monks that devastated cities and were capable of such pernicious acts as butchering the philosopher Hypatia. The indeterminate boundaries of the mystical event, its proximity to the odd and bizarre, the subterranean and unknown, give it a tarnished reputation. The majority of philosophers, from Xenophanes to Bertrand Russell, regarded mysticism — or what they thought to be mysticism — with frank distaste. Mystical writers responded in kind, savaging the philosophers and their wild pretensions.

Nevertheless, some of the greatest philosophers in the ancient world were not loath to enter a realm that strikes us as remarkably similar to that of the mystic. Plato, through the mouth of Socrates in the *Phaedrus,* discusses the different forms of *theia mania,* the God-given state of being beside oneself. The "highest goods" come to humans in the manner of *mania,* seen as a sort of divine gift. Christians who encounter the Sybil in the *Dies Irae* linked with King David testifying to the End Times would have been astonished to find her lumped together with the prophetess at Delphi and the priestess of Dodoma as examples of *transport prophetique,* public ec-stasy. According to myth, Apollo breathed into the Sybil "the riches of spirit," a state of inspiration in which self-possession is suspended, a *theia mania* that can appear as madness.

Platonism entered Christianity under many guises — exercising a strong influence on spirituality, as witnessed in the works of the church fathers, Augustine being a prime example. The Greek term for the vision of God was *theoria* (contemplation), the most elevated human activ-ity. During the third century — prior to the advent of mo-nasticism — the Christian thinkers of Alexandria (Clem-ent and Origen) applied Platonic language to the journey of the soul of God. Some Christians, then and later, re-acted unfavorably to what appeared to be a foreign intru-sion. Several centuries later, the Orthodox saint Gregory Palamas was hardly an exception when he remarked that the writings of Greek philosophers are like "poisoned snakes from whom doctors succeed in deriving useful drugs."[1]

If Platonism became a problem for Christianity, Christianity was no less a problem for Paganism. The first mention of Christianity was made by Pliny, the Roman governor of Bithynia (Turkey), at the beginning of the second century. Christianity, in his opinion, was a "superstition." Later in the century, Celsus wrote that Jesus himself was a magician and sorcerer and that Christians practiced magic and consorted with demons.[2] The Pagans in general saw the Christian community as peculiar and anti-social, a small religious sect that drew its adherents from the lower depths of society. Indeed, the number of Christians in the early second century was minimal — probably less than fifty thousand — in a society of approximately sixty million.

Criticism of the new sect burgeoned. For Tacitus, Christianity was the enemy of mankind, an affront to the religious and social world.[3] Porphyry, the editor of Plotinus's *Enneads* and his biographer, defended Pagan practices and beliefs, attempting to prove that Christianity had jettisoned the worship of the universal God in favor of the worship of Christ. Emperor Julian (The Apos-

1. John Meyendorff, *A Study of Gregory Palamas* (London: Faith Press, 1964), p. 132.

2. Robert Louis Wilken, *The Christians as the Romans Saw Them* (New Haven: Yale University Press, 1984), p. xvi.

3. Wilken, *The Christians as the Romans Saw Them,* p. 66.

tate) used the law to curb Christian influence. In A.D. 363, the Christians were forbidden to teach Greek literature because he believed that *Paideia* was a gift from the gods which Christians had abused, thus blaspheming the gods. This composed the gist of his work *Against the Galileans,* a work now lost and known to us only through St. Cyril's *Contra Julianum.* Julian had been initiated into the cults of Cybele and Mithra, and followed the line initiated by Celsus that Christianity is an apostasy from Judaism that, without scriptural warrant, has installed a "new law" and deserted the "Jewish Law" for "a new and strange rite dreamed of by Jesus' followers with no claim to antiquity."[4]

In spite of violent invective, persecution, and the dogged persistence of Paganism after the reign of Constantine, Christianity grew and prospered. It harbored the notion of contemplation as a somewhat suspect "secret sharer" and suffered a transformation in the work of Augustine, who grudgingly accepted the Neoplatonic concept of contemplation most completely. Augustine gave a different name to the terminology he accepted: "The Incarnation, taken in all seriousness, could suffice to turn such Platonism, like a glove, inside out."[5]

A short time later, Cassian taught that contemplation

4. Wilken, *The Christians as the Romans Saw Them,* pp. 149-62. Refer to Peter Brown, *The World of Antiquity* (New York: W. W. Norton, 1988), p. 934.

5. Louis Bouyer, *The Christian Mystery,* trans. Illtyd Trethowan (Edinburgh: T&T Clark, 1990), pp. 206, 209.

arises from meditation on Scripture. It is through constant meditation, supplemented by ascetic practices, that the heights of contemplation can be attained. Later, the Greek notion of contemplation waned, due perhaps to the progressive eclipse of the Greek language in the West. Marcus Aurelius (121-180), so emphatically Roman, wrote his thoughts in Greek. Over two hundred years later, the use of Greek diminished to such a point that the Emperor Julian (332-363) sponsored a revival of Hellenism, which died in the West after the emperor's death. In the East, however, Justinian was the last emperor that spoke Latin, either in public or in private. The last Greek pope was Zacharias (741-52), who translated Gregory's *Dialogues* into Greek. His successor, Stephen II, was the first of the line of purely Latin popes.

St. Jerome was one of those rare Romans of the period who could understand spoken Greek. He had followed the lectures of Didymus the Blind at Alexandria. In the fifth and sixth centuries, when few Christian writers in the West understood Greek, such translators as Jerome and Rufinus, and later Dionysus Exiguus and the group of translators at Vivarium, took on the burden of cultural exchange. The ascetic ideal, which was more authentically Christian than the transports of the Hellenic sages, found its highest expression in monasticism. Augustine, although impressed by the *Life of Antony,* did not flee to the desert, although in his community at Hippo Regius the discipline was monastic in spirit.

When Constantine entered Rome in A.D. 312, he found that the Christian church in the West had only just emerged from severe persecution. The first general prohibition of Pagan worship came in 391-92, but it would be centuries before it began to penetrate the vast mass of the population. Between 429 and 439 alone, 150 laws were passed against Pagan worship, but, at least down to the eighth century, a large segment of the population retained its fealty to some form of ancestral paganism. To make matters worse, most of the barbarians that invaded Roman lands during the fifth century had previously been converted to Arianism. Even under the severe code imposed by Emperor Theodosius II (401-50), a Pagan revival took place. In the alpine diocese of Trent, missionaries attempting to persuade converts not to participate in Pagan rites were murdered.

The Pagan revival was aided by the disasters that rocked the nascent church. The sacking of Rome by the Vandals in A.D. 410, perhaps the most spectacular, was lamented by St. Jerome: "The city is taken which took the whole world . . . the fury of the hungry sought out horrible food."[6] About two years later mobs in the streets shouted that God had deserted his people, that he had ceased to care for humanity. In the Abbey of St. Victor, puzzled Christians came to Cassian asking how God could permit

---

6. Cited in *The Conversion of Western Europe,* ed. J. N. Hillgarth (Englewood Cliffs, N.J.: Prentice-Hall, 1969), p. 67.

the death of righteous monks at barbarian hands. The church fought back with a number of condemnations. The Council of Auxerre proscribed practices such as dressing as a stag or calf on the Kalends (the first) of January, and consulting soothsayers and augurs. The privileges of the church increased, monastic vows were enforced, laws on marriage were modified, and laws against magic and sodomy were strengthened.

Both the East and the West contributed to the formation of Christian spiritual life: the desert, the monastery, and, to a lesser extent, the cathedra. The *Life of Antony* was the most famous biography of the era, and by A.D. 400 he was already a hero of the past. This volume was later joined by *The Life of Pachomius,* whose monastery at Tabennisi was notable for its size and discipline. His rule was translated into Latin by St. Jerome. Collections were quickly assembled describing the lives of the early Eastern hermits: The *Apophthegmatia ("Sayings of the Egyptian Fathers")* and its Latin translation, the *Adhoritationes,* which, when merged with a larger collection, came to be called the *Vitae Patrum ("Lives of the Fathers").*

The monastic movement advocated by Athanasius and the letters and treatises of Jerome was furthered by the authority of Augustine in Africa, Martin in Gaul, Paulinus of Nola, and Ambrose in Italy. Strange to say, monasticism was not very popular with the ruling classes, some of whom did not hesitate in denouncing the monks as "irresponsible" and "bizarre wretches," accusing them, often with provocation, of desertion and insanity.[7] Though the origin of monasticism is to some extent hidden by the fog of centuries past, the first known history of the movement is found in Cassian's *Eighteenth Conference,* placed in the mouth of Abba Piamun:

> When the Apostles died, believers grew lukewarm and converts brought heathen habits into the Church. Those who wished to continue the apostolic way of life left the towns and retired to remote country places and began to practice privately what the Apostles intended to be common practice. They separated from the body of the Church, left their families, abstained from marriage, and because of their solitude began to be called MONKS. They led a common life and were called *coenobites,* communities which perdured for a time prior to the day of Abba Paul and Abba Antony, the first hermits.[8]

Whether or not this account should be taken at face value, it can serve as a general outline to be completed by further scholarly investigation.

Mysticism seems to be the preserve of the hermit, the monk, the person withdrawn from the cacophony of the

7. Owen Chadwick, *John Cassian* (Cambridge: Cambridge University Press, 1968), pp. 34-35.

8. Chadwick, *John Cassian,* p. 51.

8

everyday world, a lover of solitude and silence, a man or woman of intense prayer. The obscurity of the mystic, his hidden life, compounded with traits which simply do not make sense to the everyday world, add to the impression that the mystic is something of a monstrosity: a person of intense prayer, quiet, silence, solitary, disciplined, conforming to Scripture, a friend to remote and solitary places. About the fourth century, the Greek word *monacho* gave birth to the Latin *monachus,* a Christian who is, at least in some respect, a solitary. The aura of otherworldliness surrounds him, the rambling along little-known paths. The desert did not disappear but was displaced to the human soul, which became a sort of counter-world: Silence, not chatter; obedience, not self-will; contemplation, not the kaleidoscopic chimeras of the imagination; detachment, not abandonment to things.

This is certainly not a program that would be followed by most practical men of letters, no matter how religious. The majority of people have often equated the mystic with the psychotic, the neurotic, the nihilist, or the voluptuary. This is true of many "self-proclaimed" mystics. The Spanish *illuminados* are a good example. To Father Francisco Gutiérrez, the Divine Essence was revealed in the form of an ox; and Father Mendez of Seville bequeathed the gifts of the Holy Spirit to his followers. However, although few persons of practical ability and worldly interests are found among the mystics — far more occupy cells in mental health establishments — there exist rare exceptions. We propose to study four of the most prominent and historically relevant of these, men who can, without undue exaggeration, be called mystics. These exceptions — St. Augustine, Gregory the Great, Anselm of Canterbury, and Ramon Llull — lived in perilous times of crisis. They were burdened with work and responsibilities, often suffered from ill health, and faced innumerable difficulties. Nevertheless, prompted by the Spirit, they attained elevated levels of spirituality.

Emperor Theodosius died in A.D. 395, the year Augustine was consecrated Bishop at the age of forty-one, his youthful misadventures and spiritual wanderings at an end. At this time Africa was a happy exception to the precarious state of the Western Empire, enjoying a period of almost unbelievable prosperity in contrast to the other provinces ravaged by the barbarians. Inscriptions still spoke of the youthful vigor of Rome and looked forward to a new golden age. In A.D. 409, the Suaves, Alans, and Vandals, all prodded by Mongol incursions, entered Spain. The following year, Alaric sacked Rome, and in A.D. 425 Genseric and his Vandals, some eighty thousand strong, crossed from Spain into Africa. Augustine died while Hippo Regius was under Vandal siege.

One of Augustine's principal difficulties was dealing

with the Donatists, an African sect that claimed to be the "Church of the Poor." They proposed no doctrinal innovation, but claimed that the Church of Donatus was the true Catholic Church in Africa. At their most zealous they inspired a movement that mingled the ascetic and the dissolute, calling themselves *Agonistici,* and in turn being called *Circumcellions* by Catholics. They attacked Pagan festivals as well as Catholic churches, and did not shirk from murdering priests. Apart from the Donatists, whom Augustine was successful in curbing, there were also the Manicheans, a sect to which Augustine himself had once belonged. He debated with them in a lengthy polemic, followed some time later by controversy with Bishop Julian of Eclanum, the brilliant advocate of Pelagianism.

Moreover, Paganism was still very much alive. By the third century, in spite of Christian advances, most towns (as well as town councils) in Africa were dominated by Pagans. Emperor Julian was a popular figure with both Donatists and Pagans, who celebrated jointly when Julian granted freedom of worship to the former. However, Christianity asserted itself, and in 421 the vast complex of Tanit — together with Baal-Hammon, the principal deity of Carthage — was destroyed, and thousands of urns containing the burnt bones of children were found.[9]

Rutilius Claudius Namatianus, in his *Itinerary from*

9. B. H. Warmington, *Carthage* (London: Robert Hale, 1960), p. 130.

Bordeaux to Rome (416), wrote a stunning eulogy of Rome precisely at the moment when its stature and might were heading for an irreparable fall. One could use this date profitably as the dividing line between the world of Augustine and that of Gregory the Great. Though the reign of Justinian (482-565) signaled an upward turn — his generals Belisarius and Narses recovered North Africa and much of Italy, and established a foothold in Spain, and Justinian himself carried out a major codification of Roman law — it was to be a brief victory. Classical culture suffered a sharp decline, and though there were exceptions such as Procopius the historian (himself something of a scandalmonger) and the architectural marvel of Hagia Sophia, the downward tilt proved too strong to resist. The schism between Orthodox and Monophysite worsened, while the population of Rome after the Gothic Wars decreased to a small percentage of its former number. Shortly after the death of Justinian, the Lombards, under Alboin, entered Italy and captured Milan in September 569.

Pope Gregory I (540-604) lived in an era in which the institutions of society had collapsed. As Bishop of Rome, he was obligated to take up a heavy burden. He was responsible for vast territories in Southern Italy and Sicily. Gregory's able administration of the church properties helped shape the machinery of the medieval papacy and the accompanying recognition of its authority in the West. Pope Gregory was responsible for the conversion of Britain, structured its hierarchy, and endorsed the *Regula Monachorum,* either the Benedictine Rule or one closely allied to it. He engaged in controversy regarding the status of the resurrected body with Patriarch Eutychius of Constantinople and spent many years attempting to resolve the schism of the Five Chapters. His relation to the Emperor Maurice was marked by mutual antagonism, and his disciplinary efforts chastened even the rambunctious Gallic clergy. Gregory's pontificate (590-604) can be said to mark a watershed in the shadowy period during which the Ancient World became the Medieval.

Gregory's reign was marked by famine, plague, and occasional Pagan revivals. The *Lupercalia* was celebrated. Nests of magicians and astrologers were discovered in Rome, and early in the sixth century several priests were detected with idols in their houses. Prior to his elevation to the papacy, Gregory held official posts such as Prefect of Rome and Papal Legate *(Apocrisarius)* to Constantinople. As pontiff he attempted, often successfully, to enforce discipline, having an especially difficult time with the "depraved" Gallic prelates. Much time, effort, and anguish was spent dealing with "the unspeakable Lombards." He made treaties to insure peace and even directed the movements of the Roman army when the Exarch at Ravenna, the Emperor's Viceroy, faltered, which, unfortunately, was not unusual.

The Lombards presented a heavy burden. Tacitus praised their daring and valor in battle. Velleius noted their "extraordinary ferocity." Procopius found them "faithless, shameless, and covetous . . . the vilest of mankind." The Lombards invaded Italy in 568 and established a kingdom by 590. Rome was threatened by Ariulf in 592 and by Agilulf again the following year. Gregory procured peace at his See's expense and by doing so angered the exarch and the emperor, who did not relish the pope as peacemaker.[10]

Gregory's missionary activities were constant and wide-ranging, directed toward Jews, Pagans, and Schismatics, and often combining kindly exhortation with disciplinary rigor. In Africa he helped extirpate the rebirth of Donatism; in Sardinia he prodded clergy to convert the idolatrous *Barbaricina;* in France he made strenuous efforts to correct the barbarization of the Gallic Church; in Spain he aided Recared to arrive at a *modus vivendi* with the Empire; in England "the timid Abbot of St. Andrews," St. Augustine, met with success, thus initiating the country's wholesale conversion. Inundated with work, Gregory suffered from poor health, including monumental bouts of gout. ("I am daily dying and daily driven back from death," he commented.) Nevertheless, his activity was unceasing.

10. Jeffrey Richards, *Consul of God: The Life and Times of Gregory the Great* (London: Routledge, 1980), pp. 181ff.

Anselm of Canterbury (1033-1109) lived in a less agitated world than either Augustine or Gregory. Less dangerous indeed, but also less sophisticated. The Roman Empire was but a memory and the papacy alive but troubled. England, for the most part Christianized, was a divided nation, detached from the Roman yoke. From the year of Rome 693 (60 B.C.), when Julius Caesar and Bibulus were consuls, to the sad day when Constantine III led away the last Roman troops, England enjoyed the benefits of *Pax Romana.* Bede tells us that "about 150 years after the coming of the Angles to Britain, Gregory, prompted by divine inspiration, sent a servant of God named Augustine and several more God-fearing monks with him to preach the Word of God to the English race."[11] Twelve bishops were empowered to be ordained, with those of London (Canterbury) and York to receive the Pallium.

Over four centuries later, Anselm was invested with the archbishopric of Canterbury on 25 September 1093, at Gloucester. Born in Aosta in northern Italy, he left home at an early age because of familial difficulties. Traveling through Burgundy and France, he came to rest at the Benedictine Monastery of Bec, where he entered as a

11. *Bede's Ecclesiastical History of the English People,* ed. Bertram Colgrave and R. A. B. Mynors (Oxford: Oxford University Press, 1968), XVII-XVIII, 1,26.

monk, studying under his famous compatriot Lanfranc. When Lanfranc moved to Caen in 1063 (he became archbishop of Canterbury in 1070), Anselm became prior of Bec, and in September 1078 was elected Abbot. After several visits to England on monastery business, he was invested with the archbishopric of Canterbury. At this point the small stream of his engagement in worldly affairs, previously limited to the care of monastic properties, became a flood.

It began with a series of taxing encounters: disputes concerning the recognition of Pope Urban II, concerning procedure with the papal legate, and concerning the knight service of his Canterbury tenants with King William Rufus. To escape the king's displeasure, Anselm left England, for the most part staying at Lyons with Archbishop Hugh. He then went to Rome, there defending the Latin doctrine of the Holy Spirit against the Greeks at the Council of Bari. After King William's death, Anselm was invited by King Henry I to return to England, but Anselm immediately locked horns with the king regarding the renewal of homage and the consecration of new bishops, defending the recent papal decrees against investiture and clerical homage.

In 1101 Robert of Normandy unsuccessfully invaded England. Although Anselm supported King Henry against Robert, difficulties between the two continued to escalate, with the result that Anselm went into exile once again on April 27, 1103, ostensibly to seek papal guidance.

The king seized Anselm's lands and revenues, forbidding Anselm to return to England. Intending to excommunicate the king, Anselm met Henry and arrived at an agreement regarding the restitution of the Canterbury holdings. After visiting Bec, Anselm returned to England in August 1106 and held two primatial councils at Westminster and London. In April he fell ill at Canterbury, where he died on April 21, 1109. Though his life was graced by lengthy periods of monastic seclusion, Anselm's exiles, disputes, wanderings, and efforts at stewardship and political engagement qualify him as an atypical mystic.

Ramon Llull (1235-1316) is undoubtedly the most unusual mystic presented here. Augustine dealt with the crisis of a crumbling Roman Empire and a Christianity attempting to find its place in a Pagan world. Gregory faced a church attempting to save remnants of civilization crumbling from within and under attack from without. Anselm's burden was the secular hubris attempting to despoil the church of its privileges and reduce it to a mere appendage of the state. Llull faced the crisis of his age — Islam and Islamic-inspired cults that flourished on Christian soil — though he attempted to counter them in what many saw as a bizarre way: through apostolic work based on his discovery of what he called "the Great Art."

His youth was hardly a pious one. He engaged in sensual pursuits (something for which he reproved himself in an early work, *Libre de contemplació*). He then experienced the unsettling vision of the crucified Christ, which was repeated five times. This was followed by a sermon on the life of St. Francis, which impressed him greatly. He decided to change his life, sold part of his holdings, and went on pilgrimage to Santiago de Compostela and other holy sites. Later, while on retreat at his property on Mount Randa, he believed that he received a revelation, the unique method of thinking and writing that has come down to us as the first *Ars Magna* ("the Great Art"), a method that Llull believed was applicable to all questions of knowledge, questions that Llull enthusiastically began to unravel.

This peripatetic propagandist bombarded the most influential personages of his day — kings, popes, princes, the intellectual elites — with constant pleas favoring the Art. Inspired by it himself, he became a Christian missionary, obtaining authorization to preach the Gospel in synagogues and mosques of Aragon. He extended the field of his activity into Africa and even, according to legend, to uncharted territories as yet unknown. Llull's strategy was to convert the "infidels" and then, in a reflex movement, purify and transform Christianity, restoring it to a perfected state. Attempting to blunt Islamic influence in Christian Europe, he launched repeated attacks on the Latin Averroists, which at first went unheard but would later fructify in the Lateran Council's condemnations of 1511.

Introduction

Though Llull was, on the whole, unsuccessful, he was able to count very prominent individuals, though often not very admirable, as his admirers. Among them was Philip le Bel of France, avaricious nemesis of the Knights Templar, and Arnau de Vilanova, who triggered great, if ominous, expectations among Christians by predicting the imminent appearance of the Antichrist. Though Arnau was considered a heretic and savaged philosophy vigorously, he still believed Llull to be a leader in the spiritual transformation of Christianity.

Llull was a man of extraordinary, though bizarre, intellect whose writings spanned literary categories. He wrote both large volumes and short treatises, and also used fables, poems, and other genres to proclaim his views. He employed the Art in a number of ways, from his discovery of it on Mount Randa to his last work on the subject in 1308, the *Ars generalis ultima.* Doubtless, in spite of the fact that he dealt with a multiplicity of themes, all can be reduced to spirituality, which was his central interest.

The "Great Art," he believed, would be able to rectify human reason and prepare the way for the establishment of a universal Christian republic. He was certain that although the world was badly damaged, it still revealed God's presence, and that if it was transformed, mankind could be restored. Two brief works that were incorporated into his mammoth novel *Blanquerna* manifest different aspects of his spirituality.

Introduction

Llull's books were many, his activity nonstop, his talks continuous, his enthusiasm contagious. Nevertheless, he can be ranked as a failure. His plans, long-term or otherwise, either were disregarded or went awry. His constant appeals to prominent figures remained unrewarded. Even his cherished Art was pushed aside and viewed as peculiar. It remained for future centuries to re-establish his reputation when he became the icon of several important philosophical and mathematical sects. What is remarkable, then and now, is that in a time of crisis he was able to rise above it, shed the multitude of activities it demanded, and ascend to the contemplation of God.

These four men — a Third Order Franciscan, a bishop, an archbishop, and a pope — were thinkers and writers who exercised, in vastly different ways, great influence on European thought and policy as well as on the history of spirituality. Augustine alone set the course of future speculation with masterpieces such as the *Confessiones, De Civitate Dei,* and *De Trinitate,* works that coursed through the lifeblood of Christianity. In Christopher Dawson's words, "The spirit of Augustine continued to live and bear fruit long after Christian Africa had ceased to exist; it entered into the tradition of the Western Church and molded the thought of Western Christendom."

Gregory, very much influenced by Augustine, wrote

works which were more practical and less intellectually sparkling, such as the *Magna Moralia,* the *Liber Regulae Pastoralis,* and the charming, fable-like *Dialogi,* which influenced the discipline, spiritual life, and imagination of the medieval church, providing inspiration to generations of Christians.

Anselm of Canterbury built on the groundwork laid by Augustine and Gregory, pioneering a new direction in religious thought by formulating what was later known as the "ontological argument." In works such as the *Monologion,* the *Proslogion,* and *Cur Deus Homo?,* Anselm gave a valuable interpretation to the Augustinian *credo ut intelligam.* His meditations and prayers influence Christian worship to this day. Anselm was considered *Augustinus minor* by his age, and even three spurious works attributed to Augustine included texts taken from Anselm.[12]

Ramon Llull introduced a new way of thinking and approaching God with a method that stood halfway between geometry and symbolic logic. He was able to enlist other genres under the banner of Art and produce works that in time gathered a goodly number of disciples and showed the beauty and majesty of God from a novel perspective.

12. The *De Vita exemitica ad sororem, De Diligendo Deo,* and *De contritione cordis.* Refer to Eugene Portalie, *A Guide to the Thought of St. Augustine* (Chicago: Henry Regnery, 1960), pp. 74-75, 352-53.

Introduction

It remains to inquire how the lives and works of these four men were able to attain to elevated heights in the life of the spirit and arrive at episodes of contemplation in which they broke through the containing walls of worldly interests to arrive at the summit of spirituality without adopting the life of a solitary, a hermit, or any other variety of person detached from the interests, pleasures, and obligations of worldly humanity. They proved it was possible to live in the world and not be immersed in it, no matter how onerous their duties or sustained their activity.

Chapter 2

St. Augustine

A UGUSTINE'S background is not impressive. He was born in Tagaste, a small Numidian town in North Africa, in A.D. 354. His father, Patricius, was a pagan, and his mother, Monica, a zealous (perhaps over-zealous) Christian. He was educated primarily in the African cities of Madaura and Carthage. As a young man he was vividly impressed by Cicero's *Hortensius*, which inspired him to lead a life of philosophy, an aspiration that became dormant as he grew older. Nevertheless, he joined the Manichean sect and taught rhetoric at Carthage, Rome, and Milan. There his disenchantment with the Manicheans increased due to his fascination with St. Ambrose's sermons, a fascination that turned him in the direction of Christian Platonism.

He became a catechumen in 385, and the following year he retired with family and a few friends to a country estate near Cassiciacum, near Milan, where the *tolle lege* conversion incident took place. The following year he was baptized by St. Ambrose. Returning to Africa, he attempted to live a community life as a "servant of God" and was consecrated a priest in 388, "against his will." In 395 he became bishop of Hippo. After a spectacular and multifaceted career, during the course of which he founded a monastery, wrote songs, attended many councils and synods at Carthage and Milevis, engaged in public debate, preached regularly at Hippo, Carthage, and Girta, and produced lasting and brilliant works, Augustine died on 28 August 430, during the siege of Hippo by Genseric's Vandals.

When Pope Urban II proclaimed the First Crusade at Clermont, he declared that Africa had been held by the enemy for over two hundred years. He insisted that this made the "danger to Christendom all the greater because it nourished the highest spirits: men whose works will keep the must of age from Holy Writ as long as the Latin tongue survives."[1] This praise of Africa, a term first used by the poet Quintus Ennius, was in great part due to the sterling reputation of Augustine.

Augustine's Episcopal see, Hippo Regius, was in his day an ancient town with streets paved by the Phoenicians, a large forum and public bath, and a classical temple on the site of a sanctuary dedicated to Baal-Hammon, one of the titular gods of Carthage along with the goddess Tanit. They were identified with Saturn and Juno by

1. R. W. Southern, *The Making of the Middle Ages* (New Haven: Yale University Press, 1980), pp. 70-71.

the Romans, whose gods, those of Olympus, were uniformly unpopular with the Africans. Even after the triumph of Christianity, the old gods counted with a large number of adepts.

Roman-African civilization was unusually brilliant. It numbered talents such as Terence (c. 159 B.C.), the Latin comic poet who wrote six surviving comedies based on Menander; Apuleius (c. 2nd century), author of the classic *Metamorphoses* or *The Golden Ass,* a satire on the vices of the age; Tertullian (c. 220), a convert to Christianity and leader of the rigorist Montanist sect, the first writer to produce major Christian works in Latin; and Arnobius (c. 330), also a convert and a rigorous defender of Christianity. Despite the passing of the centuries, the memory of Hannibal's extraordinary heroics endured, a source of both pride and resentment. Prosperous when the remainder of the Roman Empire was ravaged by the barbarians, the great majority of Africans were sanguine — disgracefully so, according to such critics as Salvian.

African humanity was idiosyncratic, its oddities exacerbated by the fear of malignant forces alien to mankind. Augustine himself believed both in the devil and in the existence of sinister ties between demons and men. Africans were noted for their surgical use of sarcasm and irony. Their lawyers were reported to be the sharpest and most devious in the Empire. Their expertise in law and statecraft was even acknowledged by Aristotle, who cited their constitution with approval and praised their institutions.

Augustine was very much an African. He shared their love of the dramatic, the intensely observed minute detail, as well as their sense of the ridiculous, which made Africans excel as writers, builders, and artisans. Exaggeration, flair, intensity, drama, the primacy of sight over the senses, of brilliant light over muted hues, and of insight over argument characterized Augustine and many of his fellow Africans. Like his countrymen, he delighted in wordplay, puns, rhymes, riddles, eccentric turns of phrase, and vivid and far-fetched similes.

The African Christians doted on miracles, martyrs, and relics. In 416 Orosius brought the relics of St. Stephen to Africa and inaugurated the custom of building chapels *(memoriae)* to house the dust of holy bones, a place where the Christian could put himself in touch with the energy-charged body of a saint, the privileged receptacle of divine grace. Of course, there was a negative side to the African personality. Disposed to alcoholism, they were also attracted by magic, auguries, and astrology. In addition, they delighted in the theatre, the arena, and the pleasures of the flesh. Augustine was no stranger to "the fleshpots of Babylon," at one time faulting himself for living in "a hissing cauldron of lust."[2]

Augustine was probably of Berber extraction. His mother's name — Monica — was possibly derived from a local deity, the goddess Mon. Though it is unlikely that he

2. Augustine, *Confessiones,* III, 1, 2; ccxxvii, 57-58.

spoke anything but Latin, his speech was burdened with an unmistakable African accent. To his brilliant young adversary, the Pelagian bishop Julian of Eclanum, he was the "Poenus," the African. He enjoyed a privileged insight into the peculiar foibles of Africans — for example, envy, then considered to be an African vice, which was later transferred to the clergy. He emulated his compatriots in other less noxious ways: fearing the sea and detesting travel and bad weather, especially winter.

He traveled from the "fleshpots" to the severity of his episcopal community by way of several intermediate stops, the most important being his nine years as an adept of the Manichees. He was impressed by the importance — even reverence — with which the sect endowed light. The Manichean god was the "Father of Light" and reigned over the Kingdom of Light, itself subtle luminous matter. Because of the original plunder of the precious substance (light) from God by an alien force, light and darkness were intermingled. The human task is to recover the stolen particles of light and eventually separate Light from Darkness so as to restore the original state of things, the Kingdom of Light.

Augustine's later enthusiasm for Neoplatonism confirmed his interest in light, though now with a greater leaning toward the immaterial, which necessarily influenced his notion of spirituality. A glance at his works proves as much. In the *Confessiones*, Augustine speaks of the "true light" which Tobias, Isaac, and Jacob, all blind

27

or nearly so, saw in their hearts. Later he points to John the Baptist and John the Evangelist as examples of men who possessed the light. Light is here identified with the requisite disposition for the contemplation of Wisdom, that light which enlightens every man coming into the world (John 1:9). At the summit dwells the supreme light, God, who we do not see but who is approached through our neighbor, whom we do see. Our own light becomes visible and leads us to the immutable light, the Light of Midday, who dispels the Night of the world.[3] Aiming at the Manicheans, who believed that plants can think, Augustine maliciously suggested that if reason were absent, the human soul would have the same status as a tree.

Robert Grosseteste, the medieval Bishop of Lincoln, continued Augustine's line of thought by affirming that among all bodies "light is the best, the most delectable, the most beautiful . . . that which constitutes the perfection of corporeal things: God is the 'first light,' the luminous and incandescent center."[4] Several medieval thinkers also followed this path. It should be stressed that "light" for Augustine is also a call to move inward, thus providing the key to what has been called, perhaps oversimplistically, the "Augustinian method" — that is, moving from external to internal, from lower to higher.

3. Augustine, *Tractatus in Iohannis evangelium,* 1, 18, 19; ccxxxvi, 10-11.

4. Robert Grosseteste, *Hexaemeron,* ed. R. C. Dales and S. Gieben (Oxford: Oxford University Press, 1990), pp. xix-xx.

Following the exigencies of light, the human soul nourishes itself, gathers momentum, and moves toward the Eternal Light. In order to attain vision of the light, the soul must be ravished by the light. The mystical state is gratuitous, a gift from God and the culmination of the process of ascent.

Augustine's speculations on the *beata vita* and the vision awaiting the blessed in the afterlife coursed through the centuries, influencing a multitude of souls, including like-minded prelates such as Pope St. Gregory the Great and St. Anselm of Canterbury. Nevertheless, Augustine has suffered from serious criticism, both in his day and down through the ages. Perhaps the most amusing, if not the most acute, came from Faustus, Manichean bishop and former associate, who maintained that Catholicism was a bizarre amalgam of Christianity and Judaism, an unsavory meld, comparable to the mixture of man and horse: Catholicism and its champion, Augustine, were *hippocentauri.*[5]

The debt to Platonism was immense. Augustine read the treatises of Plotinus translated by Marius Victorinus and was greatly impressed by Victorinus's conversion to Christianity. Porphyry, in *De Civitate Dei,* acquired the status of the anti-Christian polemicist *par excellence.* Augustine adopted and adapted many Neoplatonic terms to

5. Refer to M. Tardieu, "la foi hippocentaure," in *Saint Augustine,* ed. P. Ranson (Paris, 1988), pp. 58-66.

fit his speculations: the soul, its twofold "weight," the dialectic of *magis esse* and *minus esse* (which are nicely adumbrated in Porphyry's *Maxims*). Moreover, the method of interiorization, the psychology of the outer and the inner man, and the use of erotic language to describe higher realities proceed from the same source. It would not be outrageous to assert that both the *Confessiones* and *De Civitate Dei* were written under the inspiration of Plotinus and his followers.

Initiated into Neoplatonic speculation at Milan by Bishop Ambrose (albeit a Christian-tinted version), his early enthusiasm became muted when he attempted "Neoplatonic meditation." This initiated a process by which Augustine turned away from Neoplatonism and to Orthodox Christianity: Platonic "recollection" was replaced by Augustinian "illumination." The mixture of praise and disenchantment which marked his mature view of Neoplatonism is found in *De Civitate Dei* (VIII-X), his last extensive commentary on the subject. It is not without interest that the tenth (X) book is considered by Father Bouyer as "the last word of Augustinian mysticism . . . which directed the whole construction of this City."[6] Perhaps it would be better to consider it a sort of Prolegomenon that sets the stage by establishing the general principles of Christian spiritual life. The move away from

6. Louis Bouyer, *The Christian Mystery*, trans. Illtyd Trethowan (Edinburgh: T&T Clark, 1990), p. 209.

strict Neoplatonism is noticeable in works that Augustine wrote after the first flush of his enthusiasm had passed. He was uncomfortable with the proliferation of irrational elements in later Neoplatonism: oracles, auguries, magic, and theurgy. Augustine distanced himself through variations in emphasis and perspective, arriving at an awareness of the implications to spirituality of major Christian doctrines such as *creatio ex nihilo,* the Incarnation, and the Trinity.

Augustine's experience at Ostia while conversing with his mother, Monica, something of a contemplation "a duo," was a *novum* in the history of Christian spirituality. It was "sudden," "fleeting," a foretaste of the afterlife vision of God, not very different from the experiences described by Plotinus in *Enneads,* which Augustine considered to be genuine, rare moments when union with the One is experienced.[7] Because of this he found it necessary to distinguish between the usually lengthy and laborious process of cleansing the soul to dispose it for contemplation — a taste of vision — and those unique episodes in which the soul is temporarily taken out of itself. Augustine would have liked these "glimpses," lights along a darkening highway, to become full visions, but was resigned never to know more than the glimpses.

The magisterial *De Trinitate* barely mentions the "ecstasies" and "transports" of popular Neoplatonic ac-

7. Plotinus, *Enneads,* V, 1, 2; VI, 9, 4.

counts. Following First Corinthians (13:12), Augustine speaks of seeing God face to face as the goal of Christian life, as it comprises the eternal plenitude of joy.[8] It is not the purpose of rational activity to engender authentic contemplation. It is Jesus Christ, the Lord and Mediator, who shepherds the "Just" to the contemplation of God the Father at its most elevated as a vision of the Trinity, in whose image we are created. Ultimately, God will be *omnia in omnibus,* and the Blessed will chant an eternal canticle. To recapitulate: spirituality has Christ as its point of departure, the Trinity as its final goal, and contemplation as the bridge between the human and the divine.

In this life we love God through faith and through hope aspire to the joy of vision. The path leading to this goal is thorny and takes place by stages, "growing daily in perfection," a journey in which the weight *(pondus)* of the will is displaced from the temporal to the eternal, the visible to the invisible, the carnal to the spiritual. When the image of God is perfected in the human image, the goal has been attained and the vision of God enjoyed. The perennial aspiration of the pagan philosophers, of happiness (blessedness), hinges on Jesus Christ and not on noetic gymnastics.

Augustine uses the metaphor "palate of the heart," developed from meditation on the Psalms and Johannine texts, perhaps borrowed from Origen (c. 254), who wrote

8. Augustine, *De Trinitate,* I, viii, 17.

of a "spiritual palate" that needs to be sensitized. The Word of God is so supremely sweet that all other savors appear repugnant. He suggests that the *palatum cordis* must be healthy to be able to receive God's love and "taste" the sweetness of the Lord. In commenting on Psalms 30 and 61, he speaks of it as a "function" which the "impious" lack. In the *Tractatus in Iohannis* and the *Epistulum ad Parthos,* the healthy "palate of the heart" is viewed as the spiritual organ by which the believer tastes the "bread of God." Franz Posset believes that this might be the origin of the medieval habit of positing a distinct faculty as the locus of the human relationship to God: the *acumen,* the *scintilla,* the *potentia obedientialis,* and the receptive capacity for grace.[9]

Dom Cuthbert Butler, who lauds Augustine as the Prince of Mystics, indicates that for Augustine in this life "some beginnings of contemplation are possible, some glimpse or intuition of divine things . . . though contemplation in the full sense belongs to the next life."[10] Contemplation can be anticipated to some degree in this life. Dom Cuthbert indicates two texts he considers important for the understanding of Augustine's view of the intellectual vision of God: *De Quantitate Animae* (XXXIII)

9. Franz Posset, "'The Palate of the Heart' in St. Augustine and Medieval Spirituality," in *Augustine: Biblical Exegete,* ed. F. Van Fleteren and J. C. Schnaubelt (New York: Peter Lang, 2001), pp. 254-57.

10. Dom Cuthbert Butler, *Western Mysticism* (London: Constable, 1926).

and *De Genesi ad Litteram* (XII). The first text describes a *scala paradisi* of seven steps. The soul, grounded in its superiority to the physical world, takes up the task of purification and moves through the first four levels, arriving at the fifth step, where it discards all impiety and comes into possession of itself.

It then progresses to the sixth step when it moves toward God, the contemplation of truth, finally arriving at the seventh and final step: the fruition of the Highest Good. It is that breath of eternity which is no longer a step *(gradus)* but an abode *(mansio),* the highest and most holy of "mansions." In *De Ordine II,* Augustine sets forth a plan of studies for those most resolved to seek God with all their strength, following the precepts of the "best" life, which reaches its acme with knowledge of the Trinity.

Book X of *De Civitate Dei* sets the stage for Augustine's contemplative flights. It is a prolonged attack on Neoplatonism with Porphyry as the principal target. It begins by praising Porphyry for being aware that the human soul cannot arrive at happiness — the life of blessedness — except by participating in the light of God, the Creator. But Augustine castigates him for practicing "sorcery" and "theurgy" to attain a specious "purification." Porphyry does not realize they are impostures of malignant spirits and demons who appear to us in the form of gods and who are incapable of purifying the human spirit. It is the founder of the Holy and Most Glorious City who is the "giver" of the "life of blessedness."

Augustine castigates Porphyry for his pride, for lacking the humility necessary to accept the Incarnation, the supreme instance of divine grace. While Porphyry searched fruitlessly to find a "universal way" to the soul's liberation, one both divinely inspired and the common property of all mankind, his pride refused to let him see that the Christian religion is precisely this "universal way." The Mediator came in the flesh, and his Apostles openly disclose what in previous ages had been "veiled allusions." As the Savior took upon himself "man in his entirety," the Christian does not have to seek purifications for the three Neoplatonic components of the individual — the body, the intellect, and the spiritual soul.

Christianity is the right path, the "universal way" that leads to the vision of God and to eternal union with him. It only remains to advance further and trace, as far as possible, Augustine's journey into the thickets of mysticism proper. Christian mysticism, as we have seen, begins and ends in Jesus Christ. As Augustine states in the *Confessiones,* "Through the latticed net of flesh He attended to us . . . inflamed us; and we are fast upon His scent . . . when He appears we shall be like Him, for we shall see Him as He is. It is ours, Lord, to see Him as He is; but our moment is not yet come."[11] But this "moment" is the culmination of a process, a painful journey in which the "inner eye" of man is healed so he may glimpse at the

11. Augustine, *Confessiones,* XIII, 15, 357-65.

sun. This will be clear if we recall the hymn to the Word in the Prologue to the Gospel of John (1:1-18) and the final words of the third chapter of 2 Corinthians (3:18):

> We all reflect, as in a mirror, the splendor of the Lord; there we are transfigured into his likeness from splendor to splendor; such is the influence of the Lord who is Spirit.

The summit of human blessedness is the full vision of the face of God.[12] We may ask, How is it possible for the "human heart," which is an abyss, to ascend to this vision? In an early work, the *Soliloquies,* Augustine claims that "with one mind we may together seek knowledge of our souls and of God."[13] He seems to be visualizing a communitarian vision of God. But on the primary, the individual level, a "breakthrough" takes place when the trinitarian soul seeks the Trinitarian God without lapsing into the temptation of distancing itself from the Cross of Christ.

As A. Louth suggests, a nice expression of this quest is found in the second half of *De Trinitate.* He considers it an exercise in *fides quaerens intellectum* (faith seeking understanding), which determines how the soul arrives at the

12. *Proslogion* 26, Corbin edition (Paris: Editions du Cerf, 1986), pp. 283-87.
13. Augustine, *Soliloquies,* I, xii, 20.

contemplation of the Trinitarian God.[14] Man himself is a trinity of *mens, notitia,* and *amor* — memory, understanding, and will — and can be reintegrated into his archetype, the Triune God, by the Augustinian Method, a method described by Louth as one of withdrawal and introversion.

In *De Trinitate* XIV, Augustine again considers what is involved in the perfection of the image of God so as to purify the human soul and enable it to arrive at contemplation. The soul's facilities have the natural tendency to remember, know, and love itself, and, once the barrier presented by the Fall is removed, is then able to remember, know, and love God. In this clinging to God the human image is perfected and comes to the contemplation of the Trinitarian God. As Augustine indicates,

> When its clinging to Him has become absolute, it will be one spirit with Him . . . the mind will be raised to the participation of His being, truth, and bliss. . . . In that being, joined to it in perfect happiness, it will live a changeless life and enjoy the changeless vision of all that it will behold.[15]

This spiritual metamorphosis takes place on an individual level. But the social or communitarian level that Au-

14. A. Louth, "Augustine," in *The Study of Spirituality,* ed. C. Jones, G. Wainwright, and E. Yarnold (New York: Oxford University Press, 1986), pp. 139-41.

15. Augustine, *De Trinitate,* XIV, xiv, 20.

gustine ultimately aspires to, the true *vita socialis sanctorum,* will be realized only in the City of God, the New Jerusalem. The perfecting of the image of God in the soul entails its return to God, a radical movement away from darkness — "the land of unlikeness" — and toward the eternal light.

Chapter 3

Gregory the Great

P OPE St. Gregory the Great (A.D. 540-604), the first pope of that name and the last of the four doctors of the Latin Church, was born in Rome, the son of a wealthy patrician, Gorganus, and a pious mother, Silvia. Because of his father's status, it is most likely that Gregory received a "formal classical" education in Rome and may have studied law, as the city was still the center of legal studies. He was extremely well-read, familiar with the Latin Patristic writers (and to some extent the Greek Fathers translated into Latin), as well as classical Roman writers such as Cicero, Vergil, Seneca, and Juvenal. In 573 he was made Prefect of Rome, pictured by Gregory of Tours "in silken robes sewn with glittering gems."[1] Later, upon withdrawing from this post, he founded seven monasteries, six on family property in Sicily, and one (the Monastery of St. Andrew, noted for its rigor) in his house on the Caelian Hill.

---

1. Jeffrey Richards, *Consul of God: The Life and Times of Gregory the Great* (London: Routledge, 1980), pp. 26-27.

He was ordained a deacon in 578 and left St. Andrew's when he was appointed Apocrisiarius (Papal Legate) to Constantinople by Pope Pelagius II. While there he made the acquaintance of the Spanish bishop, Leander (elder brother of Isidore of Seville), and began work on his exposition of the Book of Job, which was later published in thirty-five volumes and dedicated to Leander under its new title of *Magna Moralia.* Gregory also found the time to engage in a polemic with the patriarch (Eutychius) regarding the states of the resurrected body.[2] His position was that it would be palpable, not insubstantial, as Eutychius proposed. The clash became bitter, to the point where the emperor himself intervened and decided in Gregory's favor, decreeing the burning of Eutychius's tome on the subject. The aftermath of the acrid debate was enough to cause the patriarch to drop dead in front of the emperor. Gregory himself, though the winner, became severely ill.

Recalled to Rome about 586, Gregory was given the delicate task of negotiating with the Istrian schismatics. In 590 Pope Pelagius died, and Gregory was elected pontiff. After a lengthy, eventful, and historically momentous pontificate, during which Gregory was burdened with physical and psychological disabilities, Gregory died on 12 March 604, with Rome still in danger from without and in the grip of famine within. But Rome would survive, for

2. Richards, *Consul of God,* pp. 38-39.

Gregory had provided its strongest institution, the church, with a future through his life, work, and writings.

Rome was the centerpiece of Gregory's life. St. Andrew's, later his home, was not far from the Baths of Caracalla, which at its peak accommodated 1,600 bathers. It was deserted, dry since 537, and now populated only by vagrants. The Flavian Amphitheater, the Coliseum, was in fairly good condition, but like the Circus and the Thermae, it was no longer used for gladiatorial contests. Gregory enjoyed the "vast library" of his relative Pope Agapetus (535-36), where he became familiar with the works of St. Augustine. The writings of the African saint made more than a passing impression on the young Gregory. The fire of Platonic mysticism, passed like a torch from Plotinus to Augustine, would flare up again in Gregory's sermons.[3] That Rome was still of paramount importance at this time is nicely illustrated by a verse from the Venerable Bede, when he notes that, when Rome falls, the world shall fall with her.

By Gregory's day, Rome had radically deteriorated from her previous majesty. Romans lived among decaying monuments, giving the appearance of a funereal city claustrophobically encased within the famous walls built by the Emperor Aurelian (271) — walls that were believed by its population to be totally unnecessary. Gregory of

3. Peter Brown, *The World of Late Antiquity* (New York: Thames & Hudson, 1989), pp. 133-34.

Tours' *History of the Franks* gives a clear and quite depressing picture of the Eternal City at this time:

> In the previous year, in the ninth month, the river Tiber had covered the City of Rome with such floods, that ancient temples fell down, and the granaries of the Church were destroyed, with the loss of several thousand bushels of wheat. A multitude of serpents swam down the course of the river to the sea, among them a great dragon. . . . A pestilence soon followed, which men call the plague of the groin. . . . It first of all attacked Pope Pelagius . . . and swiftly quenched his life.[4]

The Rome of Gregory was a far cry from the Rome of the Golden Age. It was literally a world without order, a world of horrors, ruled by demons, witchcraft, miracles, and wonders. Despite this environment (and his many endeavors), Gregory was able to write in profusion: serious books, such as exegetical works on Job, Ezekiel, the Song of Songs, and 1 Kings; popular works, such as the *Dialogues* and *Homilies on the Gospels;* over 850 letters; and lost works on Proverbs, the Heptateuch, and the Prophets.[5]

In addition to the maelstrom that was Rome, the

---

4. Gregory of Tours, *The History of the Franks,* Vol. II, bk. X, chap. I.

5. Carole Straw, *Gregory the Great: Perfection in Imperfection* (Berkeley and Los Angeles: University of California Press, 1988), p. 6.

pope was also responsible for vast territories in southern Italy and Sicily. He governed these with a deft touch. As R. L. Wilken indicates, Gergory's administrative gifts were unusually sharp for a cleric.[6] While for the vast majority of his predecessors the break between the practical and the religious, the carnal and the spiritual, was deep and wide, Gregory saw direct links between them: they interrelate and affect each other, often profoundly, yet often in ways that strike us as rather comical. The *Regula Pastoralis* postulates that a crooked nose denotes excessive subtlety, a hunchback is dragged down by earthly cares, and a person with a broken foot or hand cannot walk the way of God. His mix of the profound and the trivial is further evidenced by the contrast between the profundities of the *Moralia*, the practical expertise of his letters, and the credulous tales of the *Dialogues.*

Doubtless, Gregory has been misunderstood to some extent, but this is the usual fate of an enigma. He has been called everything from a Stalinesque dictator to a mediocre combination of tiresome moralities and reflections. However, it is best to avoid these extremes and view Gregory instead as he was: a very talented, very spiritual prelate with outbursts of genius and acidic temper; Orthodox, but for his era hardly a fanatic man. In Constantinople he witnessed outbursts of "fanatical orthodoxy," leading him

6. R. L. Wilken, *The Spirit of Early Christian Thought* (New Haven: Yale University Press, 2003), pp. 312-13.

to observe that "many orthodox people who are inflamed with misguided zeal . . . fancy they are fighting heretics while really they are creating heresies."[7]

The most important dichotomy for Gregory is that between the Inner World, where peace is to be found, and the Outer World, where there is distress and disturbance. The external is linked with the visible, cold world of the flesh; the internal with the invisible, warm life of the transcendent spirit. The human soul should move toward a participation in the life to come, which is one of unalterable stillness, a peace which is both light and silence. Gregory attempted to lead his flock in this direction by example, exhortation, and discipline: he sent visitors to oversee Episcopal miscreants such as Bishop Andrea of Tarentum, who stole, ill-treated his clergy, kept concubines, and reportedly beat an indigent woman to death. Gregory also defended the right of sanctuary as a means of pursuing justice for the innocent and urged bishops to avoid secular involvement except in defense of the poor. His policy was to protect monasteries from Episcopal domination, and he sanctioned the sale of church treasures for charitable purposes. On the first of the week he distributed produce collected from his rents (corn, wine, meat, fish, and oil) to the poor. Cooked rations were sent daily to the sick. Even dishes from his own table were sent to the poor. In addition, he made generous bequests.

7. Gregory, *Epistles,* XI, 27.

Paul the Deacon related that Pope Gregory's successor, Sabinianus, refused to continue his "lavish charities." Gregory appeared to him three times in a vision, warning him to repent. As this did not produce a change in Sabinianus, Gregory appeared to him a fourth time and struck him on the head with his staff. Soon after, in February 606, Sabinianus died.

The reign of Justinian provided the background for the early life and later accomplishments of Pope Gregory, and what may be considered the most important events of his life: the Lombard invasion, the Schism of the Three Chapters, and the conversion of England. Justinian succeeded his uncle as emperor in August of 537 and immediately proceeded to shore up Christianity through legislation, much of which bordered on the harsh. His generals, Belisarius and Narses, were effective throughout most of their campaign. Justinian himself, prodded by his notorious spouse, Theodosia (herself a sexual and literary legend), put down the "Nika" revolt in the capital. The Arian Vandals in Africa were defeated, Sicily was conquered, and Italy itself was invaded, against strong Goth opposition. The Goths were defeated and their king, Totila, was killed. The Pragmatic Sanction of 554 reorganized Italy as a Roman province governed by an exarch, who resided at Ravenna. Not all accomplishments were military. Justinian abolished the famous pagan School of Athens, making education definitely Christian, and introduced silk manufacture, long a closely held Chinese secret, to the West. Perhaps his most lasting contribution to civilization was his ordering and codifying of Roman law, the *Digest* (*Pandects* in Greek), known as the *Corpus Iuris Civilis* since the sixteenth century. Unfortunately, as if to balance the scales, Justinian's interference in ecclesiastical matters and indirect support, through Theodosia, of the Monophysite schism would sow the seeds of future mischief.

The emperor's last days were anticlimactic. In December 557, when Gregory was seventeen years old, a great earthquake shook Constantinople, and in the following year the dome of the Hagia Sophia, his architectural *pièce de résistance,* collapsed. The plague, which had been devastating the city intermittently, returned to claim more victims in 565. These events seemed to be a harbinger of the future: a mere three years after the death of Justinian (568), the Lombards invaded Italy and by 590 established a kingdom. Agilulf took Pavia in 593 and appeared at the gates of Rome, where Pope Gregory was preaching homilies on the prophet Ezekiel. Gregory immediately interpreted the advance of the "abominable Lombards" as another sign of the approach of the End Times, an attitude strengthened by seeing his fellow Romans being led away into captivity, bound with chains like dogs. Although his efforts at concluding a peace treaty with the Lombards (through the good offices of Theodelinda, the Lombard queen) eventually succeeded, Gregory, disappointed by the exarch's failure to act, took over effective command of Rome, supervising the military operations. The Lombards did not disappear but continued to cause mischief for another two hundred years, up to the time of the fall of Desiderius (774). During this period they scuttled the Arian Christianity to which they had been converted and embraced orthodox Catholicism.

Gregory saw the End Times — the release of Satan and his incarnation in the Antichrist — on the near horizon. The "signs of power" would be withdrawn from the church and a new church would be founded: that of the Reprobate. The Evil Spirit, acting in concert, would attack the minds of men with its "numbing" power. This sense of immediacy is powerful. According to Carole Straw, "Gregory saw apocalyptic signs foretold by Jesus (Luke 21:25-33) being realized all around him."[8] Most unsettling is a recurring vision he described: two "mystical bodies," one divine, one demonic, wending their way through the centuries to the End Times and their ultimate destiny in heaven or hell. Throughout, Gregory used the language of "Incarnation" when speaking of Satan's historical appearance as the Antichrist.

If the Lombards provided a material obstacle to Gregory's pastoral activity, the "Three Chapters" (or Istrian schism) did so on the ecclesiastical level. Three Syrian bishops — Theodore of Mopsuestia, Theodoret of Cyrrhus, and Ibas of Odessa — were condemned about a century after their deaths because Justinian was persuaded that the

---

8. Straw, *Gregory the Great*, pp. 51-52, 55.

"germs" of the Nestorian heresy were contained in their works. Justinian believed this condemnation served to mollify the Eastern dissidents, which was essential to his bringing about imperial unity. Pope Vigilius, cowed by imperial pressure, readily approved the stipulations of the Fifth Council by condemning the Three Chapters. For many in the West, however, this condemnation was seen as a betrayal of the gains made at the Council of Chalcedon, and unsettlement was great, with Paulinus, the patriarch of Aquileia, leading the resistance together with Pelagius. The latter changed course and was elevated to the pontificate as Pope Pelagius I. When Gregory became pope, he followed the example of Pope Pelagius II, arguing that Chalcedon must have *implicitly* condemned the three, since it approved of Cyril and the Council of Ephesus, which they had opposed.

Gregory sent a copy of Pope Pelagius's letter to each of the schismatic bishops, inviting their consideration. He also wrote a brief but rather acerbic letter to the Patriarch of Aquileia lamenting his departure from "the way of truth" to no avail, as even his friend, Queen Theodelinda, was opposed, consenting to the protests of three Suffragan bishops. In effect, Gregory skirted the question by noting that whatever had been done in the time of Justinian did not impair the authority of Chalcedon. The result was that the schism was not squelched, but continued to fester until about 698, when, during a council at Pavia, the representatives of Aquileia were restored to the unity of the church. It was duly commemorated by a rude poem: *Carmen de Synodo Ticinensi.*[9]

Perhaps the best way of introducing Pope Gregory's mission to Britain is to quote its great historian, the Venerable Bede:

> In the ninth year of the Emperor Maurice, who ascended in 582, Gregory, a man eminent in learning and affairs, was elected pontiff of the apostle see of Rome. About 150 years after the coming of the Angles to Britain, Gregory, prompted by divine inspiration, sent a servant of God named Augustine and several more God-fearing monks with him to preach the word of God to the English race.[10]

The party landed on the "Isle of Thanet" and, after early miscalculations, was able to convert the King, Aethelbert (married to Bertha, a Christian). Augustine was consecrated "Archbishop of the English race" at Arles. Faced with new situations, he wrote to Gregory for help. Gregory's answer came in the form of his *Libellus Responsionem.* He reversed his previous stand that the temples of the pagans should be destroyed. In a letter to Abbot

9. Thomas Hodgkin, *The Barbarian Invasions of the Roman Empire,* reprint (London: Folio Society, 2000), vol. 5, p. 304n.

10. *Bede's Ecclesiastical History of the English People,* ed. Bertram Colgrave and R. A. B. Mynors (Oxford: Oxford University Press, 1968), XVII-XVIII, I, 26.

Mellitus, Gregory declared that only the idols in those temples should be destroyed. As for the temple itself, "take holy water and sprinkle in these shrines, build altars and place relics in converting the shrines from worship of devils to the service of the True God."[11] Christian festivals should be celebrated joyously, so that by outward rejoicing the people would more easily share in inward rejoicing.

The impetus for Gregory's missionary activity may well be depicted in the account given in the *Whitby Life,* perhaps the earliest piece of written literature produced by Anglo-Saxons. The meeting of Gregory with the English youths in the Roman marketplace and his famous series of puns told that the men of the kingdom were called "Deiri." Gregory laughed, "'De Ira' — good! Snatched from the wrath of Christ and called to his mercy." When told that the king's name was Aelle, his response was "Alleluia! The praise of God the creator must be strong in these parts." The author of the *Whitby Life* was a Northumbrian living when Edwin was "our King" and Paulinus was "our teacher."

Pope Gregory was also a subject of myths, several of which, including Trajan's liberation from hell (later commented on by St. Thomas and Dante), became famous. The British continued to venerate Pope Gregory as the Apostle of the Island for centuries. The *Dialogues* and the *Regula* were paraphrased by King Alfred the Great. St. Adhelm, writing a few decades prior to the Whitby monk,

11. Gregory, *Epistles,* I, 30.

spoke of Gregory as a teacher and instructor who took away the error of heathenism and replaced it with regenerating grace.[12] The Council of Clovesho (747) confirmed his status by decreeing that Gregory's "dies natalis" — the date of his birth into heaven (March 5) — should be celebrated with a solemn festival.

Gregory was, in spite of himself, very active. His reign was inaugurated by a massive litany to deliver Rome from the plague. Seven processions met at the Church of Santa Maria Maggiore. The pope preached, the people prayed aloud, and eighty people dropped dead. Gregory's pastoral care extended to the corrupt clergy of Gaul, the vicissitudes of political fortune in Spain, and the elaborate maneuvers of Constantinople. His character, thoroughly conservative and authoritarian, leavened with a sarcastic sense of humor, often struggled with his virtues, a struggle that often led to unfortunate incidents, providing a glimpse into the pontiff's darker side.

Perhaps his most famous lapse was his reaction to the deposition of the Emperor Maurice and the "unholy glee" with which he greeted the news of his death, especially as

12. The *Whitby Life* is the earliest life of St. Gregory and was written by an anonymous monk. Text, translation, and notes are by Bertram Colgrave (Lawrence, Kans., 1968), pp. 1-2, 46, 29, 127-29. St. Thomas questioned the veracity of the Trajan story (*Summa Theologica*, III, q. 71, a. 5). Dante refers to it twice (*Purgatorio*, X, 73-93; *Paradiso*, XX, 106-17). In the last version Trajan comes to life to declare his Christian faith.

his successor, Phocas, was a disaster, a degenerate who forced Maurice to watch his four younger sons butchered before beheading him. Maurice's three daughters were placed in a convent only to be executed in 605 on suspicion of conspiracy. It is entirely possible that the pope was not aware of the circumstances surrounding the emperor's death. Yet there were many prior incidents that might explain such a harsh reaction: Gregory's protest against an edict forbidding public servants to enter a monastery, and his defense of Archbishop John of Prima Justiniana, whom Maurice accused of disloyalty, presumption, prodigality, and stupidity. Gregory's reply to the emperor came in the form of a sarcastic, rather arrogant letter. But no matter how irked Gregory became, it would not excuse his reaction to Maurice's murder if he had been apprised of the circumstances.

Although Gregory could wield a bitter pen — his sarcastic letters to John the Faster are good examples — he could also, if occasion demanded, drip treacle. He was criticized for his caressing letters to Brunhild, the "second Jezebel," with whom he established contact in 595 and corresponded in ten letters. The once beautiful, high-spirited, ambitious woman was also described as "a woman of passion, plots, violence, and intrigue."[13] At her instigation, Bishop Desiderius of Vienne was stoned to

13. F. Homes Dudden, *Gregory the Great: His Place in History and Thought,* reprint (New York: Longmans, Green, 1967), pp. 12-14.

death and St. Columban expelled from Burgundy. This was hardly a momentary weakness of the pontiff, but rather a strategic ploy, as Brunhild controlled the fate of Austria and Burgundy through her wards, the boy-kings. Gregory's influence with her ended with her unfortunate demise: she was tortured, tied to the tail of an unbroken horse, and dragged to her death.

The only incident that should be added to this catalogue is Gregory's rigid interpretation of the monastic rule of poverty. The monk-physician Justus, dying, confessed to keeping three pieces of gold. Gregory forced the monk to die alone and threw his body and coins on a manure heap, saying, "Take your money with you to perdition" (Acts 8:20).[14] Although this punishment and his intercession were said to have procured Justus's release from Purgatory, the response strikes us today as excessively harsh. Augustine, facing a similar situation, was more sympathetic. But Gregory was a neophyte to the monastic life and was intent on the strict interpretation of his Rule, which, it seems, was more rigorous than the Benedictine Rule, to which he must have made some minor modifications. However, Benedict himself insisted that the *Magister Regula* and the *Sancta Regula* were to be obeyed absolutely, even above the abbot.[15]

14. Gregory, *Dialogues,* 4.57, 9-11. Refer to Straw's comments, *Gregory the Great,* pp. 47ff.

15. Dom John Chapman, O.S.B., *St. Benedict and the Sixth Century,* reprint (Westport, Conn.: Greenwood Press, 1971), pp. 12-13, 25-26.

It would seem the Gregory was sunk in the morass of the active life without respite: administration, preaching, politics, diplomacy, discipline, controversy, and national and personal tragedy. His realization of this is seen in the mournful tone of his correspondence immediately after assuming the pontificate. He did not relish leaving the silence of the monastery. To Theocista, sister of the Emperor Maurice, he wrote,

> I have lost the deep joys of my old quietude . . . internally I am in a state of collapse . . . I am driven from the face of my Creator . . . the most serene Emperor has ordered an Ape to become a Lion. A Lion, indeed it may be called at the Imperial Command, but a Lion it cannot become.[16]

When he later wrote the *Dialogues,* the central character was St. Benedict, his famous vision found in the second book (patterned after Macrobius's *Commentary on the Dream of Scipio*). It is perhaps the most famous non-biblical vision in the Early Middle Ages and illuminates Gregory's teaching on contemplation as both a goal to be attained and a pattern to be followed. The individual must jettison cares and worldly attachments so as to fly in contemplation.

16. Cited by Hodgkin, *The Barbarian Invasions of the Roman Empire,* vol. 5, pp. 185-86.

In Benedict's vision the world is gathered together before his eyes: the "interior light" of the mind allows the person rapt in God to see everything that is beneath him. This privilege is attained only by a "patient climb," an image that became popular among later monastic writers: Anselm, Bernard, and Richard of St. Victor among them. The contemplative life demands much mental struggle to rise toward the heavenly, to narrow in order to expand and perceive a glimpse of that eternal freedom "which eye has not seen, nor ear heard" (1 Cor. 2:9). The goal is "to see God," and we can move forward to this goal by progressing in contemplation.[17]

Given his position and duties, it is surprising to note that Gregory spoke of mystical contemplation and experience in far more detail than did his predecessors. The theme fascinated him, as did the reality. Perhaps it is because contemplation is the antidote to the innate human impulse to sink below oneself, enabling the soul to move to higher levels. But even at the highest level, "repelled by the weight of its own mortality, it falls back to the depths." This *reverberatio* has a family resemblance to Bonaventure's *vertibilitas,* the natural downward gravity of the human soul. But the upward flight itself should be moderated through humility. One can "go astray" by dwelling too long on the unseen, or by seeking corporeal light in the incorporeal. In any case, as contemplation is

17. Gregory, *Magna Moralia,* 8.49.

brief and fragile, one can mount the *scala considerationis* and step by step ascend from visible creation to invisible reality.

Though mankind's ultimate goal is "to see God," Gregory indicates that prior to the vision itself there is a *visio per appetitum* in which the mind enjoys a "savor," a taste of the satiety it will enjoy in the future. The goodness is tasted before it is achieved. Making use of a "chink" or "slanting window" of the understanding, the soul is able to overcome the resistant shadows and attain a glimpse of the Light of Truth. Contemplation is not always filled with light. Gregory believed that dread — that of Job (Job 4:14) — can be generated by awe of the darkness of contemplation. Confronted by this abyss, our security and self-assurance liquefy, a strong rejoinder to the usual picture of Gregory as a "mystic of light," since powerful negative theology underlies his thought.

Gregory followed tradition by distinguishing between two lives, the Active *(Vita Activa)* and the Contemplative *(Vita Contemplativa).* The Active precedes in time, while the Contemplative has greater merit as it already tastes future rest. The Active deals with morality, and the Contemplative deals with immortal life. The object of understanding Scripture is conversion, which culminates in the life of contemplation. At its apex, the contemplative is full to overflowing, his mind illuminated by brilliant light — a light that itself is life — while savoring the inner sweetness.[18] The Active and the Contemplative are not hermetically sealed domains. Frequently a man passes to the Contemplative without abandoning the Active.

Contemplation is the end of the road. One travels from faith to vision, from belief to contemplation, under the guidance of patience and humility. Gregory advised that one should humble oneself before everyone, inasmuch as one does not know who among us may be Christ. Moreover, the Spirit can change the human heart in an instant, filling it with light. We are no longer what we once were; we are something we never used to be. The contemplative becomes a new creature and in doing so imitates the resurrection of Christ.

Gregory believed that humanity's "fatherland" is the terrestrial paradise where man possessed the grace of contemplating God: Adam, he contends, was a contemplative. Unfortunately, because of the Fall, it is impossible to go home again. The Incarnation of the Word makes the return to the fatherland, otherwise impossible, a possibility. The lost order can then be restored. At present we can offer our minds as a "holocaust" to God in contemplation, to arrive at the True Light:

Where the light so encircles us outwardly that we are filled inwardly and so fills us inwardly that being limit-

18. Gregory, *Homilies,* III, 9, 13. *Magna Moralia,* 5.34.12; 30.5.18; et al.

less it encircles us outwardly . . . souls are illuminated by this light of the living, and they perceive it the more clearly the more purely they live according to it.[19]

Where does the path that leads to contemplation begin? What prods or impulses led Gregory in that direction? The Monastery of St. Andrew was greatly influenced by the Benedictine Rule, to which he refers several times, although it was not in general use in Italy in the sixth century and not until the tenth century was it exclusively used by the monasteries of Rome.[20] St. Benedict made reading a central part of monastic life. Four hours daily were assigned to *lectio divina,* and it was the chief occupation of the monks on Sundays. (In *lectio divina* words are "sampled" so as to release their savor and weighed in order to capture the full depth of their meaning.) Moreover, religious reading was a spiritual exercise, a synthesis of *Lectio Divina* and *Meditatio.* The two are inseparable.

Although encountered on the heights as the flowering of meditation, contemplation also plays a role on a more pedestrian level. The *Liber Regulae Pastoralis,* which was enjoined, together with the New Testament and the Canons of the Fathers, by councils held under Charlemagne, is a good example. Basically a manual for bishops, in this work Gregory speaks of some persons

19. Gregory, *Magna Moralia,* 24.12.35.
20. Chapman, *St. Benedict and the Sixth Century,* p. 253.

having a hidden place of quiet reserved for contemplation. In this way they are able to serve their neighbor without the blindness that afflicts those unacquainted with contemplation. Gregory states that even the ruler, who should be a "near neighbor" to everyone in sympathy, should be exalted above everyone in contemplation.[21] Contemplation does not desert the external, the carnal, but allows one to consider the "secret things of God" without being suffocated by it.

It is important to note that almost all of the later vocabulary of the West concerning the spiritual life has its origin in Gregory's assimilation and rewriting of the vocabulary of Cassian and Augustine. This is probably related to the vision of the two monks at Benedict's death, of the magnificent road taken by Blessed Benedict on his way to heaven. Gregory exemplified what Bernard of Clairvaux stated when he discussed the different kinds of monastic contemplative:

> He is greatest of all who, having dissociated himself from the use of things and from all of the senses . . . has formed the habit of flying off on occasion in contemplation to the sublime . . . not by gradually ascending stages, but by unexpected departures.[22]

---

21. Gregory, *Liber Regulae Pastoralis,* V, 4-5; II, 8, p. 9; II, 5, pp. 12-14.

22. Clairvaux, *De Consideratione,* 5:3, vol. 3, pp. 468-69.

In effect, Gregory distinguished the properly contemplative episodes from the laborious intellectual ascent by the *scala considerationis.*

The process begins with meditating on Scripture, the nourishment of prayer. As Gregory indicated, it is a matter of coming to know "the heart of God."[23] Scripture is God's letter to his creatures. Gregory advised meditating daily on the Creator's words so as to yearn more ardently for things eternal, thus mingling the world of the supernatural with that of ordinary experience. The carnal then become signs, mediating links between this world and the transcendent. Sacrifice is of the utmost importance, as it is the means by which the two sides of reality — the carnal and the spiritual — are joined and reconciled, with the carnal becoming spiritual. His notion of *consideratio* is related as, by this process, not only is the inner man examined, but also his outward actions. Ambrose employed it in *Isaac vel Anima* several years prior to Gregory.[24]

This indicates that the appropriation of the spiritual sense of Scripture was at the center of the monastic piety transmitted to the Anglo-Saxons by Gregory in the 597 mission and by travelers to and from Rome in the seventh century. This type of piety become so ingrained in the British mind that several kings chose to die in Rome: Caedwalla of Wessex in 689, and Conrad of Mercia and

23. Gregory, *Epistles,* IV, 31.
24. *Dialogues,* 3.7; Straw, *Gregory the Great,* pp. 19-20.

Offa of Essex in 709. The emphasis on the spiritual distinguishes Gregory from a great bibliophile such as St. Isadore of Seville, who used one of Gregory's homilies on verses from Luke, clearly stressing moralizing passages, while Gregory emphasized the spiritual, the "inner articulation" of the "new man." A later writer, Valere du Bierzo, influenced greatly by Gregory, followed in his steps, calling solitude the touchstone of the monastic vocation, prayer and asceticism its most important aspects.

Gregory declared that "the Lord's commandments are both many and one: many through the variety of works, one in its root, which is love." The practical teaching was never far from his mind: A person truly possesses love who loves his friend in God and his enemy for God's sake. Love, ardent desire for eternal life, is that "love as strong as death" which Solomon praises (Song of Sol. 8:6). As death destroys the body, so ardent desire for eternal life cuts off love of material things. And this is possible because a divine person took on the weakness of the body and recovered the light it had lost.

The sixth-century view of the great majority of mankind, overwhelmed by wars, plague, natural disasters, and a multiplicity of other ills, was scarcely optimistic. Pope St. Gregory reflected this view. Man is born amid the hardships of exile, coming here with a feeling of loathing. This is a negative spin on Augustine's idea of the "resident alien." In keeping with this view, authority — the subjection of one man to another — does not belong to the primitive order of things, but is rather the consequence of sin and is the providential means of bringing men back to God.[25]

In the religious sphere this century brought certain novelties. As Peter Brown indicates, "The written word had withdrawn into a shell. Music was the new form of the Sixth Century.... The cross was now charged with the Crucified and the Icon . . . the stylized portrait."[26] Moreover, a gulf opened, separating the religious and the secular cultures in a way that earlier Christianity could not have envisaged. Of the many myths that have surrounded Pope Gregory, one that still retains its freshness is his contribution to church music, Gregorian chant in particular. The Venerable Bede is wrongly attributed with connecting Gregory with plain chant. Bede only mentioned two bishops who learned church music in the Roman manner from disciples of Gregory. However, by the eleventh century the legend of Gregory's connection with the chant crossed the line from fantasy to fact.

If his contribution to religious music was apocryphal, his contribution to Christian spirituality, to mysticism, was not. That Dom Georges Lefebvre, in his *Priere Pure et Purete du Coeur,*[27] can present parallel texts from Gregory and John of the Cross that culminate in a section ti-

25. *In Ezekiel,* I, 6.

26. Brown, *The World of Late Antiquity,* p. 181.

27. Dom Georges Lefebvre, *Priere Pure et Purete du Coeur* (Paris, 1953).

tled *Avant-Gout du Ciel* is a good indication of his stature. No doubt Gregory, exile in this world, is sorrowful, but it is the platform from which the soul ascends toward something far better, when "we will share with the blessed spirits in pure Creator's glory, we will see the face of God before us and behold Infinite Light."[28]

28. LeFebvre, *Priere Pure et Purete du Coeur,* pp. 81-82.

Chapter 4

Anselm of Canterbury

A NSELM can only be understood as a man dedicated to, and perhaps obsessed with, the monastic way of life. More than either Augustine or Gregory, he directed his energy to the observance of the Rule of St. Benedict even after his elevation to the archbishopric of Canterbury. Overburdened with work and disputes that caused his exile several times from England, Anselm enjoyed only brief periods when it was possible to retreat into himself and encounter the Trinity within. His exterior activity — practical, intellectual, and ecclesiastical — made him one of the major figures of the age, together with Pope Urban II and William the Conqueror.

At first glance, compared to the times of Augustine and Gregory, the period in which St. Anselm was born seems to have been a sanguine one, when the great events that formed medieval Europe had subsided. However, on closer inspection, we find this to be far from the case. The age in which he was born (the eleventh century) had different protagonists. The major figures were

Abbot Odilo of Cluny and Pope Benedict IX, the first a monument of spirituality, the second a man with a reputation as a monster of perversity. When Anselm died in 1109, Cîteaux and Chartreuse were challenging the supremacy of Cluny. Pope Paschal II reigned. The founders of organized scholastic thought, scholars such as Anselm of Laon, Abelard, Gilbert of Poitiers, and others were moving from place to place gathering adepts and renown. In the words of R. W. Southern, Anselm's life "covered one of the most momentous periods of change in European history, comparable to the Reformation or the Industrial Revolution."[1]

Anselm was born in 1033 in the alpine town of Aosta to a family related by blood and vassalage to the great house of Savoy. His father, Gundulf, was a Lombard, reputedly a spendthrift; his mother, Ermenberga, related to Count Humbert II of Maurienne, was an heiress to a small barony in the Aosta Valley. While his father engaged in business, his mother lived an intense spiritual life. The town of Aosta itself was ancient, though undistinguished, retaining many buildings originally constructed by the Romans: an amphitheatre, a praesidium, a triumphal arch, walls, and fortified gatehouses. There were also the remains of a medieval settlement, an abbey and a cathedral. In the eleventh century it was the south-

1. R. W. Southern, *Saint Anselm: A Portrait in a Landscape* (Cambridge: Cambridge University Press, 1991), p. 4.

ern outpost of the Kingdom of Burgundy, an imperial possession under Emperor Conrad II.

Anselm's intellectual progress was prodigious. At the age of fourteen he held the ecclesiastical rank of canon and was placed under a private tutor, though later he showed little interest in either law or rhetoric. When his mother died, the antagonism that existed between Anselm and his father intensified, and he left Aosta. The next few years he spent wandering. He probably visited his mother's relations in Lyons and Vienne before reaching Avranches, in the west of Normandy, where his Lombard compatriot Lanfranc, now a privileged advisor to Duke William, had taught. His next stop was Bec, where Lanfranc took him in hand.

Anselm seems to have been torn between Cluny (he was put off by its "severity") and Bec, where Lanfranc's "outstanding ability" would condemn him to insignificance. Selecting Bec, Anselm professed to Abbot Herluin in 1060 and three years later rose to the rank of prior when Duke William (the Conqueror) chose Prior Lanfranc to be the first abbot of his foundation of St. Stephen. Much has been made of the relationship between Anselm and Lanfranc, who had gained fame as a lawyer, bringing prosperity to Bec by opening a school, where, in the acidic words of William of Malmesbury, he "sent out his pupils belching forth dialectic."[2] In addition, he had

2. Cited by Southern in *Saint Anselm,* p. 17.

great ability in practical affairs and energy sufficient to put his plans into operation. Anselm, in contrast, was an intellectual prodigy completely lacking ability in practical matters. He has been nicely described as an "introspective oddity."[3]

He was twenty-five years old when he arrived at Bec. Lanfranc, aside from being prior, was already a trusted advisor to Duke William. For over four years Anselm benefitted by his example and direction, though their characters were vastly different — in some ways, even opposed. Their association was close and friendly, albeit on the level of master-pupil, which did not cease until Lanfranc's death, despite a minor setback earlier when Anselm sent him a copy of the *Monologion* and received a curt reply. In spite of his intellectual proclivity, Anselm turned primarily to the spiritual life at Bec, where "God will be to me all in all, there His love will be the only subject of my contemplation."[4]

Life at Bec afforded him time to think, meditate, and write. Intellectual stimulation was not absent from the Bec monastery. Its library contained the major works of Augustine (which became the greatest influence on Anselm's thought aside from sacred Scripture), Ambrose, and Jerome. Other works were collected or searched for,

3. Southern, *Saint Anselm,* p. 15.

4. Eadmer, *The Life of St. Anselm,* translated and edited with an introduction and notes by R. W. Southern (Oxford: Clarendon Press, 1962) I, ii, 4-5.

including St. Dunstan's *Rule,* Bede's *De Temporibus,* Galen's *De Pulsibus,* and even the *Opus Medicinae Hippocraticae.* (In fact, the first explicit reference to Aristotle in a medieval theological treatise is found in Anselm's *Cur Deus Homo?*)

He began his literary career with *De Grammatico,* a treatise on logic. After an interval of about seven years, which he spent in meditation and spiritual exercises, he began penning letters, prayers, and meditations relating to the spiritual life and directed to persons outside the monastic community. His later philosophical treatises, *De Veritate, De Casu Diaboli,* and *De Libertate Arbitrii,* were not merely scholarly treatises but also expanded and amplified meditations on biblical texts.

Southern makes a nice point when he states that "Augustine made a poetry of persuasion, Anselm a poetry of logical congruities and contrasts."[5] More to the point, both Augustine and Anselm viewed meditation as a bridge between sense knowledge and knowledge of the being and attributes of God. Their program of ascent was similar: from image to thought, thought to meditation, meditation to contemplation, contemplation to the eternal vision of God, which is the goal of all existence. Anselm injected a new intensity into medieval spirituality, which, though grounded in the corporate life of the monastery, touched the individual, moving from cloister

5. Southern, *Saint Anselm,* p. 77.

to chamber. Introspection was organized, abounding in fervor and leaving Carolingian sobriety in its wake. (The entire collection of prayers which complete the cycle of *Prayers* and *Meditations* was ultimately sent to Countess Matilda of Tuscany.)

Even the great meditations on the nature of God, the *Monologion* and the *Proslogion,* all of Anselm's writing for twenty years, developed from the introspective method of the *Prayers* and *Meditations.* The *Proslogion* was intended as a meditation for the believer and a proof for the unbeliever. The argument contained within its pages can be said to move in three stages. The first two correspond to those processes of thought that constitute *meditation,* the third to that which transcends thought — *contemplation* — which can lead to an experiencing of God's Being, itself a foretaste of the beatific vision. The very fact that the argument was received by Anselm in a moment of "joy and exaltation," after he earlier attempted to reject it as a diabolical temptation, confirms its importance. This took place in 1077. About a decade later, Anselm wrote to Hugh the Hermit (1086): "If your holiness wants to read at greater length something written by me about the fullness of eternal blessedness — you can find it at the end of my little book called *Proslogion.* There I dealt with complete joy."[6]

The year in which Anselm completed the *Proslogion,*

6. Anselm, *Letters:* Epistles #112, 268-70.

he succeeded Herluin as abbot and visited England, staying for some time with his friend Gilbert Crispin at Westminster and returning to Bec in 1081. He returned to England in 1086, seeking royal confirmation of the scattered possessions of Bec, and in the autumn of 1092 he supervised the construction of a new monastery and visited the ailing Earl at Chester. But his abbacy was more productive than these visits: 122 novices made their monastic profession into his hands during this period.

The greatest secular as well as religious movement of the age was undoubtedly the Crusades. Anselm had little sympathy with a movement that was disruptive and militated against monastic stability. Pope Urban's call to Christendom in 1095 at Clermont inspired extraordinary enthusiasm that increased when Jerusalem fell to the Crusaders in 1099 after having been occupied by Moslems since 638. Ouitremer became a reality with four great baronies: the principality of Galilee, the double county of Jaffa and Ascalon, the lordships of Kerak and Montreal, and the lordship of Sidon, together with twelve smaller fiefs.

The Templars and Hospitallers had not yet been founded. Hugues de Payens had not yet persuaded St. Bernard to compose a rule for the Templars based on the statutes of his Cistercian Order. It was duly written and popularized by the pamphlet *De Laude Novae Militiae,* a work intended to attract recruits. The disastrous Battle of Hattin (1187), which nearly destroyed the Latin kingdom, was still seventy-eight years in the future.

Obsessed with the heavenly Jerusalem and not the earthly, Anselm aspired to the celestial "vision of peace," which was possible in the monastic life. Although influenced by the Platonic tradition mediated through Augustine, he did not dismiss the physical world as mere appearance and criticized the temptation to misuse it. Nevertheless, his opinion of the "world" was not optimistic. In a dream, a vision, or, as Eadmer has it, an "ecstasy," he saw a swift and turbulent river into which flowed all the "purgings" and "filth" of the world with human beings greedily drinking the obscene brew: a striking image of the world and the worldly from a most unworldly monk.[7]

Following Augustine and Gregory, Anselm's touchstone is faith. Without faith, there is no experience; and without experience, there can be no understanding. Faith is the point of departure to arrive at an inner experience of truth situated beyond the limits of reason and which, on attaining a certain level of intensity, can be called mystical. This is the goal of the journey, the entrance to ultimate bliss, a direction Anselm has been pointing to from the very beginning of his monastic life.

Anselm added an important proviso to the role of reason as seen in his *Proslogion,* innocent of appeals to biblical authority: The Bible is present in modes other than that of "authority." Although faith is the necessary point of departure, as Edward Synan suggests, "a future failure

7. Eadmer, *The Life of St. Anselm,* I, xxi, 35-36.

in faith must leave intact a rationally secure conviction that God is."[8] This is to say that in a religious age within the monastic enclosure an area of reason — not reducible to faith — is encountered.

Monastic life was not without its problems. Two major problems, one interior and one exterior, faced Anselm at this time. First was the notion of Roscelin that Anselm supported his heretical view on the Trinity. The second concerned the Hildebrandine reforms, which attempted to impose ecclesiastical centralization and control. The latter gave him much to ponder, though he defended the papal directives as a matter of obedience. Insofar as Roscelin was concerned, however, Anselm responded vigorously some two years after he had been enthroned as archbishop of Canterbury in a scene worthy of true medieval camp.

Anselm was a poor administrator who was all too conscious of his lack of expertise. This is best illustrated by the two letters he wrote to Lanfranc, voicing his conviction that God would provide if the Rule were strictly followed. As an abbot, he was often accused of being excessively mild in disciplining his monks, though he could be quite rigorous in dealing with wayward ones. He believed that a monk living under a Rule must be held to a higher standard and subject to a stricter discipline. In

8. Edward A. Synan, "Prayer, Proof, and Anselm's *Proslogion*," in *Standing Before God* (New York: Ktav, 1981), pp. 267-88.

practice, however, he could be quite flexible in dealing with his monks, an attitude compared by some to his acquiescence in lay violence. Nevertheless, he was successful in establishing good relations with the lay aristocracy and enjoyed a remarkable hold on the affections of violent and aggressive men. Although noted for his charm and kindness, he was considered by his critics to be highhanded when he ignored precedent and chose his successor as abbot of Bec.

He was consulted by many people seeking advice or help in interpreting Scripture, from the scholar to the illiterate shopkeeper. Anyone seeking an answer was accorded his ear.[9] Jewish scholars, recently arrived in London from Mainz, had engaged his friend Gilbert Crispin in a debate concerning the Incarnation. Crispin wrote an account of it and dedicated it to Anselm, who took up the cudgel and wrote a treatise deducing the necessity of the Incarnation from the nature of God and the rational beauty of the universe. This was *Cur Deus Homo?,* in which intense emotion matches logic in the service of a rigorous spirituality: "Were it not better that the whole world, and whatever is that is not God, should perish and be reduced to nothingness, than you should make one movement of the eye against the will of God?"[10] The superiority of the monk consists in his complete submis-

9. Anselm, *Cur Deus Homo?* I, 9.
10. Cited by Southern in *Saint Anselm,* p. 230.

sion, embracing joyfully whatever restraints are demanded of him.

When Anselm became archbishop, he was wrenched from a life in which he enjoyed periods of meditation and prayer to one that burdened him with a complex web of responsibilities that had been largely shaped by Lanfranc. As archbishop and head of a monastery with claims to rights and lands, be became (in England) second in importance only to the king and second in the ecclesiastical hierarchy after the pope. The downside of his elevation came from close friends that began to ask for church lands, power, money — whatever happened to strike their fancy.[11] Because Anselm was hardly a politician at heart, this took him by surprise, as did the circumstances that brought him to the archbishopric.

When King William Rufus fell seriously ill in March of 1093, the See of Canterbury had been vacant since the demise of Lanfranc. The bishops and barons pressed the king to fill the vacancy and, after much wrangling, Anselm was forcibly invested on 6 March 1093. Almost immediately he entered into a dispute with the king over the law of *usus atque leges* of William the Conqueror, which stipulated that the Anglo-Norman rulers were supreme in both temporal and spiritual realms. Anselm resisted in obedience to the "law of God" and of the church at the Curia Regis at Rockingham in February 1095, and

11. Eadmer, *The Life of St. Anselm,* II, xiv, 81-82.

again at Winchester in October 1097. This opposition to the king drove Anselm into exile from November 1097 to September 1100, during which he spent much time with his friend Archbishop Hugh of Lyons, visiting Cluny and LaChaise-Dieu in early August. The most agreeable part of this exile was Anselm's stay at Liberi, where he occupied his mind night and day with acts of holiness, divine contemplation, and sacred mysteries.[12]

Despite the acrimony engendered by the investiture controversy and the difficulties posed by the Hildebrandine Reform and other problems, seventeen of fifty-two of Anselm's surviving letters during this period were concerned with monastic vows and discipline. Only one letter, to Hugh of Lyons, deplored the king's hostility, and this was done without rancor. Anselm sympathized with both the Hildebrandine Reform and the claim of Urban to the papacy, but he could not commit the Kingdom of England since the choice pertained to the king. He decided that if the king did not back Urban, he would leave and resign the archbishopric into the pope's hands. Unfortunately, his knowledge of papal decrees was minimal, although Dom Boso had been sent as his envoy to the Council of Clermont and had personally spoken to Pope Urban II in 1098 and 1100.[13]

Other difficulties assailed Anselm, two dealing with

12. Eadmer, *The Life of St. Anselm,* II, iv, 43.
13. Southern, *Saint Anselm,* p. 257.

aristocratic women. The first was Matilda, later Queen of England, to whom he at first addressed sharp words. But, as the difficulty was able to be resolved with only a modicum of effort, relations between the two warmed to the point where Anselm was transformed into her spiritual father. It was not to be so, however, with Gunhilda. A beautiful and talented woman, she was the last known descendent of Harold, the last Anglo-Saxon king, who was defeated and killed by Duke William at the battle of Hastings on 14 October 1066. She had entered the convent at Wilton from where she was abducted by Count Alan Rufus, with whom she conducted a torrid affair. Even after his death she had not returned to the convent. Anselm wrote her two letters which, from today's perspective, were highly macabre, telling her to "gather his worms unto your bosom, embrace his corpse, kiss his bare teeth," among other suggestions.[14] That Gunhilda returned to the Wilton convent and was remembered with honor says much for the religious temper of the day and perhaps for the efficacy of reprimands couched in macabre terms.

Anselm proceeded, but hardly at the pace he desired, to discipline wayward clerics, several of them prelates. He suspended two bishops during his first year, these being Welshmen who had retained the customs of the Celtic Church. There existed much friction in Anselm's

---

14. *Hetteus,* Epistle II, #168, 64-69; #169, 70-73.

time, not only between Roman and Celtic rites, but also between Bec and Molesmes, between Canterbury and York, through which Anselm obtained wider recognition of the primacy of Canterbury. The conflicts even extended to Canterbury itself, where the Anglo-Saxon and the Norman monks were at odds and to which the misdemeanors of the always fractious Gallic clergy could be added. The effect of these conflicts left Anselm feeling overwhelmed, so much so that in September of 1095 he wrote the following to Pope Urban II:

> Holy Father, I grieve to be what I am, I grieve not to be what I was. . . . I seemed to accomplish something in a humble place, whereas in a lofty position weighted down by a great burden produce no benefit to myself nor do I succeed in being useful to anybody. I collapse under the burden. . . . I suffer from a lack of strength, virtue, diligence, and knowledge adequate to so great an office.[15]

It was a beautiful, touching confession (not without its pragmatic undertow), which reflects the man at his best.

During his first exile, Anselm was summoned to Rome, where he attended the Easter Council of 1089 at St. Peter's. There, the bishop of Lucca pleaded for action on his case, while the Fathers imposed excommunication on

---

15. *Hetteus,* Epistle II, #193, 123.

lay investiture and clerical homage to laymen, reiterating Pope Gregory VII's condemnation of 1078. Pope Urban II died in August 1099 and was succeeded by Pope Paschal II. Anselm's absence from England had been noted in some quarters with misgivings. Pope Paschal wrote King Henry a chiding letter, expressing amazement that not only was Anselm exiled but also despoiled of the possessions of his church. To Queen Matilda he was even sterner: "He [Henry] has expelled the holy man, Bishop Anselm, from the kingdom because he opposed his wicked deeds, and taken on counselors of perdition."[16] Many of the letters commending him, especially those of Queen Matilda — a wealth of adjectival eulogy — must have been highly embarrassing to the archbishop.

On the other hand, Prior Ernulf of Canterbury reproved Anselm for his absence: ". . . allowing us to be harried by shameless and cruel enemies who spare neither our modesty nor our safety . . . the unjust and pitiless tyranny of Princes, the plundering of the poor, the despoiling of churches, to the point that even the Lord's body and blood loses its serenity."[17] Things seemed to be going from bad to worse during his absence.

Anselm returned to England on 23 September 1100, and a few days later met with King Henry I at Salisbury. When he refused to renew the homage he had given to

16. *Hetteus*, Epistle II, #352, 87; II, #193, 123.
17. *Hetteus*, Epistle II, #310, 709.

King William Rufus or to consecrate the bishops Henry had invested, the king desisted from reprisals. However, when the messenger he had sent to Rome returned with an unacceptable reply, the king demanded that Anselm comply with his wishes or leave England once again. This Anselm did, arriving at Rome to take the first steps toward the excommunication of King Henry. From December 1103 to April 1105 he attempted to justify his exile in the face of rising criticism from England.

On 22 June 1105, on the eve of King Henry's successful campaign to take Normandy from his elder Crusader brother Robert, they concluded the "Compromise of L'Aigle," which allowed the church elections to ecclesiastical offices to be carried out within the Curia Regis and left the king in control of ecclesiastical fiefs. Anselm could return to England; his lands and revenues were restored, and he was granted permission to convene councils. He fell ill upon finally returning to England in September 1106.

During the last year of his life, the archbishop held two councils, enlarged Lanfranc's church, and constructed a new building after the model of a recently constructed church at Cluny that Pope Urban II had dedicated in 1095. Although at first he shared the opinion of Lanfranc and the Normans that Anglo-Saxons were *barbari,* he later seconded Dom Boso in attempting to do justice to the Anglo-Saxon saints and restore their pieties. At an earlier date he convinced Lanfranc of the sanctity of Anglo-Saxon Bishop Elphege. He also proceeded to curb excesses such as the veneration of Earl Waldef by the community of (Anglo-Saxon) nuns of St. Mary at Ramsey. The earl was the only Anglo-Saxon of high rank to be executed for treason during the reign of William the Conqueror, and the reaction of the nuns was to be expected.

Anselm was also known for his talks and sermons concerning the monastic life. In a letter to Lanzo, a novice, he stated,

> Anyone taking a vow of monastic life to strive with total application of his mind to set down roots to live in whatever monastery he had made his profession . . . and to refrain from judging the behavior of others or the customs of the place . . . let him resolve to devote himself assiduously to pursuing the single-minded exercise of a holy life.[18]

Thirty years later he advised the monk Hugh to love his monastery life above all else, a task that could be done easily by "never wishing to hide or defend your faults." Through the Holy Spirit Hugh's good habits would drive away any wickedness and would become such a source of pleasure that "you will not be able to imagine anything more delightful and joyful."[19]

18. Anselm, *Letters:* Epistle I, #37, 135.
19. Anselm, *Letters:* Epistle II, #232, 204-5.

One of the major criticisms leveled against Anselm was that he excessively cultivated those virtues pertaining to a monk, but not to a prelate. Hence, he was faulted for a mildness which, critics maintained, was exploited by many so as to remain in their wickedness. His mildness, coupled with the seemingly amorous terms he used in his letters to the monastic community and others, has raised doubts concerning his sexuality. This seemed to take on more force with John Boswell's contention that Anselm prevented the promulgation of the first anti-gay legislation in England.[20] In reality, Anselm proposed a general council to condemn sodomy, illicit marriage, and "other wicked dealings in things abominable."[21] A meeting took place when the court met at Hastings. In the autumn of 1102 he wrote William, archdeacon of Canterbury, that ". . . by the sin of sodomy, the sentence will be one and the same if they confess and seek absolution. . . . This sin was so common that hardly anyone was ashamed of it, and many people, ignorant of its magnitude, fell headlong into it."[22] Like Augustine, he was irritated by long hair, and two canons of the Council of Westminster (12 and 23) prohibited its wearing by the clergy. Although R. W. Southern suggests that Anselm may, at most, have had a

20. John Boswell, *Christianity, Social Tolerance, and Homosexuality* (Chicago: University of Chicago Press, 1980), pp. 204, 218.

21. Anselm, *Letters:* Epistle II, p. 82, n. 4.

22. Anselm, *Letters:* Epistle II, #257, 248-49.

"homosexual disposition," this is a matter better left to psychologists.[23]

What can be criticized in Anselm aside from his penchant for morbidity (part of the atmosphere of his times) was his abandonment of Duke Robert to his fate after his defeat by King Henry I, who condemned his elder brother to life imprisonment and possibly to blindness. Moreover, Anselm's pliancy was often mistaken for weakness, and this in turn produced misinterpretations and conflicts. Anselm's sixteen years as archbishop of Canterbury were stormy, with only brief respites dedicated to monastic peace. The dispute with King William Rufus over *usus atque leges* was followed by the investiture controversy with King Henry I. Constant efforts to bring about the reform of the clergy, the proper disposition of lands and serfs, and the ancient quarrel with York regarding supremacy gave him little opportunity for lengthy periods of prayer and contemplation. In July 1108 Anselm fell seriously ill. Though he improved during autumn, his fragile health deteriorated again during the winter of 1108-09. He died on 21 April 1109, at seventy-six years of age.

Dom Jean Leclercq has done yeoman service in the history of spirituality by pointing out that from the eighth to the twelfth century it is possible to distinguish two cultures: the monastic and the scholastic. The first is a con-

23. Southern, *Saint Anselm,* p. 151.

tinuation of the Patristic Age.[24] Anselm's spirituality was intense and framed in strict logical treatises such as the *Monologion* and the *Proslogion.* While the *Monologion* is an *indagatio,* a term previously found in Gregory to describe an unremitting investigation of a troublesome problem, the *Proslogion* can be classified as a *gnosis* when viewed from the perspective of monastic culture. Étienne Gilson describes it as "that kind of higher knowledge which is the complement, the fruition, of faith which reaches completion in prayer and contemplation."[25]

Beginning in the monastic centuries, the pilgrimages to Jerusalem, Rome, Compostela, and other holy places were replaced in the monasteries by a "pilgrimage in stability" *(peregrination stabilitate),* an inner pilgrimage in which the soul endeavors to recover its original status as image of the Divine Image, acquiring a greater resemblance the closer it moves toward the Indwelling Deity. The logical gyrations of the argument serve to purify the mind and reach the conclusion that God is greater than can be thought. Then it moves toward the "sun," which, in some way, can be experienced. The *Proslogion* leads to experiencing God in hope in this life, which adumbrates

24. Dom Jean Leclercq, O.S.B., *The Love of Learning and the Desire for God: A Study of Monastic Culture* (New York: New American Library, 1963).

25. Étienne Gilson, "Sens et nature de l'argument de S. Anselme," in *Arch. d'Hist Doct. et Litt. du Moyen Âge* (1934), p. 49. See also Leclercq, *The Love of Learning and the Desire for God,* p. 215.

a superior state in the next: *experiri, experientia, experimentum* recur.

A passage of Anselm's *Epistola de Incarnatione Verbi* indicates that experience may lead to knowledge higher than that obtained by hearing. For Anselm, as for Augustine and Gregory, knowledge is directed to its completion in wisdom, and wisdom is directed to ultimate vision. That the human soul desires "to experience You" is a theme that runs through Chapters 16 to 18 of the *Proslogion,* and Chapter 23 is a rhapsodic tribute to those "sons of God" in whom the love of God generates such enormous joy that "the whole soul is not sufficient for the plenitude of joy."[26] Knowledge, love of God, and joy will be great in hope "here," and made complete "there." The life of vision is not severed from the present life but is its goal and completion. What is adumbrated in this life is made complete in the next.

The *Proslogion* is not a mystical treatise proper, radically different as it is from works such as those of John of the Cross and Johannes Tauler. It is more intellectual and less spiritual and contains a rational element not under the aegis of faith. It ends when the others reach the midpoint of their ascent; the "spiritual marriage" is not consummated. Like Moses on his lofty peak, Anselm in the *Proslogion* climbs to the spiritual heights, from which he

26. Anselm, *Proslogion,* 23, 121, 14-18: *"Tota anima suffiviat plenitudem gaudii."*

can see the Promised Land, purifying the soul so that it can move beyond reason and meditation, and, thus freed, can fly to its eternal home in Heaven.

Chapter 5

Ramon Llull

R AMON Llull was not an important figure of his age. He was neither a prelate nor a priest. He was a layman, a Third Order Franciscan. While alive he did not influence others to any great extent. Only after his death did he become the legendary discoverer of the philosopher's stone that transmuted base metals into gold, and the writer of the *Testamentum,* the famous alchemical tract. He was rejected by the greater part of the intellectual community as an unwelcome gadfly, a bizarre exception, an unflagging enthusiast, a man of strong if unusual intellect and extravagant imagination, the center of a developing mythology, an individual hyperkinetic to the point of traveling to many parts of the known world and, at least according to legend, beyond its limits.

Despite the vast reservoir of myth and legend surrounding him, it is possible to present a sketchy outline of Llull's life. His father had participated in the conquest of Mallorca, and Ramon belonged to the nobility of the island. Although in the *Vita coetánea* he says nothing about his infancy and childhood, we know that he was born in Ciutat de Mallorca (Palma) around A.D. 1235. At the age of fourteen he became a page in the service of King Jaume, accompanying him in his travels and receiving the education of a gentleman: the practice of arms softened by the graces of the "troubadour." According to the *Vita,* his youth was given over to sensuality and lust, for which he castigates himself in an early work, *Libre de contemplació.*[1]

Aside from his incursions into the regions of sexual gratification, other more permanent influences were at hand. Mallorca had become the refuge of Franciscan Spirituals, Joachimites, and Cathars. His merry way down the worldly path was halted by five visions of Christ crucified. He took this to mean that Christ had liberated him from his "carnalitat" so as to make Him known throughout the world. This conversion was intensified by a sermon Llull heard on the life of St. Francis. He then sold part of his holdings and went on pilgrimages to holy places such as Rocamar and Santiago de Compostela. He also studied Latin with the nearby Cistercians and learned Arabic from a Muslim slave (who later turned against his master, was imprisoned, and died). At the end of this period of his life, Llull wrote the bulky *Libre de contemplació en Deu,* which tilted toward spirituality. His erratic and quirky nature, combined with a noticeable

1. Llull, *Libre de contemplació en Déu,* 132, 27.

lack of practical ability, prodded his wife (with whom he had two children) to obtain an administrator of the family patrimony.

Llull would often retire to a property near Mount Randa, close to the Cistercian monastery of Santa Maria la Reial, to meditate and pray. While on retreat at Mount Randa he had an exceptional experience: God illuminated his intelligence and gave him the "form and order" for thinking and writing books. He went down to the monastery and, as stated in the *Vita,* wrote "without effort a book against the infidels."[2] This was the first *Ars Magna* ("The Great Art"), which was later developed more fully in the *Ars Generalis Magna.* The "infidels" referred to followers of Islam and Islamic-induced cults in Christendom, such as Averroism and Catharism. Llull was convinced that he and his Art could convert them. (Indeed, he was instrumental in turning the tide against Islam.)

Ars Magna, much criticized by later writers, reflected Llull's belief that it was possible to demonstrate with absolute certainty the mysteries of religion. Moreover, "the Great Art" could, without the benefit of learning and reflection, provide answers to all questions. The method consists of placing a series of nine concepts and questions on seven moveable concentric disks and manipulating the disks in such a way as to produce an answer. Llull's works on a plethora of subjects attest to the Art's

2. Llull, *Vita coetánea,* 14.

adaptability and to Llull's faith in its power. Centuries later, another great polymath, Leibniz, praised Llull, crediting him with discovering the *Ars combinatoria,* the ancestor of the computer.[3]

After three years at Miramar directing a school for the study of Arabic, alternating prayer, study, and writing, Llull initiated a public career that would span some forty years, taking him (at least in legend) beyond the limits of the known world. Armed with the Art and its exceptional powers, he scurried about, constantly imploring, advising, preaching, debating, and attempting to influence popes, kings, universities — in short, any person or institution of prestige or influence. He petitioned Pope Celestine V (the pontiff of *il gran rifuto*). He sought the assistance of Jaume II of Mallorca, and Philip the Fair (whom he praised fulsomely, presenting him with several of his books, including *L'Arbre de filosofia d'amor,* and years later dedicating *De Natali pueri parvuli Christi* to him), pleading that he suppress the Averroist heresy. Llull's judgment was often unstable, due to mood swings that often left him on the verge of psychosis.

In October of 1299 Llull received authorization to preach in the synagogues and mosques of Aragon from King Jaume II. He set off for Cyprus, stopping at Armenia

---

3. Gottfried Martin, *Leibniz: Logic and Metaphysics,* trans. R. J. Northcott and P. Lucas (Manchester: Manchester University Press, 1964), pp. 24ff.

and Limissol before arriving in 1305 at Lyon, where he was received by Pope Clement V. He then traveled to Bugia (Africa), where he was stoned, beaten, and imprisoned before being expelled. On his way to Pisa he survived a shipwreck, finally reaching the Franciscan convent of San Donnino.[4] There, his mystical inclination could have been furthered by acquaintance with the works of Gerard of Borgo San Donnino, who, in 1254, had written his *Introduction to the Eternal Gospel* — an edition of Joachim of Fiore's three major works with an introduction and glosses. This initiated a veritable epidemic of enthusiasm that was still percolating during Llull's lifetime, concentrated to some extent in the Franciscan Order. As a Franciscan, Llull must have been familiar with the substance of the Calabrian abbot's thought. The extent of its influence on him has as yet not been determined.

Returning to Paris, Llull attacked the Averroists, gave several well-attended public lectures, and, reaching the height of his success, saw his works declared orthodox by the chancellor of the university. Unfortunately, the same university issued an official document after his death, between 1395 and 1402, prohibiting the teaching of Llull's Art in the Faculty of Theology.[5] The Council of Vienne

4. Armand Llinares, *Ramon Llull* (Barcelona: Edicions 62, 1987), p. 88.

5. Llinares, *Ramon Llull,* p. 89. J. N. Hillgarth, *Ramon Llull and Llullism in Fourteenth-Century France* (Oxford: Clarendon Press, 1970), p. 269.

saw the triumph of several of the ten propositions that Llull put forth in his *Petitio Raymundi*. But his insistence on condemning the Averroists did not come to fruition until the Lateran Council of 1511.

Old age did not diminish his enthusiasm. Returning to Mallorca, Llull wrote fifteen books in less than a year. His last adventure was in Tunis, where he preached and debated with the Islamic sages. According to tradition, he was stoned by an Islamic mob and was near death when he was taken aboard a Genoese ship heading to Mallorca. He expired upon sighting the coast. Other versions of his death exist, testifying to its mystery. The most credible of these has Llull dying on 29 June 1315 on the Feast of the Martyrdom of Saints Peter and Paul.

Llull was a person unable to hold his missionary enthusiasm in check. He was compelled to preach, expounding and teaching the poetic, scientific, and literary work subordinated to the Art, which he sincerely believed was the means given to him by God to restore humanity to a perfected state. As a "troubadour," he must have been influenced by the cult of courtly love with its connections to Islam and Catharism. He often visited Montpellier, which was a gathering place for various groups of enthusiasts. Llull was acquainted with the Franciscan Spirituals and exercised his apostolate at several places frequented by them: Ifriquiya (Tunisia and part of Libya), the refuge of the Fratricelli in 1217, and the refuge of the Freres de Narbonne et de Bezier. He was aware of the euphoria produced by Arnau de Vilanova's *De Tempore adventus Anti-Chrisi et fine Mundii,* which predicted the imminent appearance of the Antichrist and strongly urged church reform. Arnau himself, though he savaged philosophy, thought highly of Llull, "the standard bearer of the spiritual reform of Christianity."[6]

A man of protean interests, Llull wrote on philosophy, theology, astrology, medicine, pedagogy, rhetoric, politics, and more. J. N. Hillgarth places him, together with King Alfonso X, as a historian presenting the most comprehensive portrait of the Iberian Peninsula in the thirteenth century. The first important writer in Catalan, he was the primary reason that Catalan preceded other European languages as a literary and scholarly medium. His principal work is almost contemporary with that of Dante and a century older than Froissart's *Chronicles,* Chaucer's *Canterbury Tales,* and Wycliffe's translation of the Bible. Like Roger Bacon, Llull envisioned and attempted to prepare the way for a universal Christian republic.

Spirituality was one of Llull's favorite themes. He moved from the lengthy, cumbersome *Libre de contemplació en Deu* to gems such as *Libre d'amic e amat* and the *Art de contemplació,* both of which were incorporated into his voluminous allegorical novel, *Blanquerna.* It responds to the exigencies of the Art, which progressed from the original Art elaborated on Mount Randa to the

6. Llinares, *Ramon Llull,* p. 39.

Ars generalis ultima (also known as the *Ars Magna*) in 1308. It is indebted to Neoplatonic tradition, channeled through Augustine to Anselm, Scotus Eriugena, and possibly al-Ghazzali (a point made by Pico della Mirandola).[7] As in the *Art de contemplació*, Llull often alternates between speculation and spiritual techniques. Beginning with the Dignities (the Divine Attributes), it proceeds to consider the created universe, love, and prayer, finishing with allegories that have over the centuries presented difficulties to interpreters.

Llull was obsessed with method, which for him was identified with the application of the Art. He discusses the method to induce contemplation, to generate love, to preach, and so forth. Father Platzeck insists that the Art itself, in its original form, was a method of inducing contemplation for personal use. Ultimately, the Art is a method by which human reason is rectified and consequently a superb apologetical tool preparing the way for the constitution of a *republica Christiana,* by means of necessary reasons.[8]

The Art revolves around God — the "A" of creation, one with his Dignities (Attributes) — which descend in a participatory manner to creation. This is to say that the Divine Attributes are reflected in the created world and the

7. Hillgarth, *Ramon Llull and Llullism in Fourteenth-Century France,* p. 161.

8. Matthias Platzeck, *Felix,* I, 12. *Sw.* 2, pp. 717-18.

extent of participation determines the degree of reality possessed by the being under consideration. Because this creation is structured in different degrees of reality and existence, everything is created *ad similitudem suarum dignitatem.* Llull advocates (like St. Gregory) a spirituality of light far distant from the dense cloud of unknowing and its tortuous way of purification. The path to God is an ascent from the perfections found in creatures, faint shadows of the Dignities, to the summit of the mount where the Dignities dwell. The ascent is not without its pain, however, as each elevation of spirit is accompanied by a quantum of suffering.[9] The more the divine Dignities inform and structure human perfection, the swifter the soul's elevation to God.

The Dignities, identified in God, are reflected in creatures in different degrees of intensity. The more the "created virtues" in man are reduced to unity, the more being/reality is possessed and the higher the soul ascends to God. On the other hand, the more man embraces evil — and hence non-being — the more he falls into Nothingness. It is the Dignities, then, that radiate through creation, drawing the spiritual man toward his transcendent goal: participation in the Trinitarian life. Though Llull depicts this ascent in geometric figures and logical forms, it is a fully human endeavor.

As mentioned earlier, the *Blanquerna* contains two rela-

---

9. Llull, *Libre d'amic e amat,* 244.

tively brief treatises dealing with spirituality: *Libre d'amic e amat* and *Art de contemplació.* They join to promote Llull's principal enterprise — that which gives life to his geometric figures, speculations, verse, and outlandish projects — that of *mending the world.* The world, albeit shattered, reveals the presence of God and, once transformed, will restore mankind to its proper status. The present chaos will be reduced to order and eventually replaced by a unity of language, customs, laws, and religions. The Art provides a method to attain contemplation, a *combinatoria* by which the divine Dignities are considered from different perspectives, a procedure that etches them on the three faculties of the soul: memory, intellect, and will.[10]

Libre d'amic e amat, in which God (*amat* — "beloved") and the soul (*amic* — "lover") are the protagonists, is an affect-inducing work similar to, and perhaps influenced by, certain Islamic practices with which Llull was familiar. It presents some 360 sayings which, when repeated with fervor, generate affect, lead to practical resolutions, bring God to mind, and induce contemplation. Through the medium of these sayings it is possible to learn to meditate and to prod the soul to higher levels of contemplation.[11] They include aphorisms, epigrams, narratives, puzzles, questions, and exclamations. These sayings are not allowed to wander freely but are subject, as is all else,

10. Llull, *Art de contemplació,* probs. 3-4.
11. Llull, *Libre d'amic e amat,* prob. 1.

to the rigor of the Art. "Infused science," acquired through acts of the will, devotion, and prayer, is not detached from "acquired science," the fruit of study and intellect.[12] The mechanism of the Art organizes, controls, and directs the effusions of affect.

A clue to the workings of his spirituality is found in Llull's great interest in its psychosomatic aspect: physical actions are closely matched by their psychical accompaniments. Affects, attitudes, posture, emotions, physical traits, and so on are signs of spiritual dispositions. For example, when the soul perseveres in meditation, the heart begins to "take fire" and the eyes "to water."[13] Llull seems to believe that these experiences are more common during upward ascents. When progress stalls, the somatic effects are muted. There are also downward movements, breaks, falls, descending spirals, when the understanding falls to the level of the imagination. Here, Llull follows the intellectualistic bent of Platonic thought in viewing the imagination as the villain of the piece, while the intellect is the culmination of human knowledge, the point of departure for supra-rational activity.

Though his spirituality is truly novel, his works contain a number of constants found in mystical literature. These include the "cloud," which in Llull is transparent; the "light" by which the Beloved illuminates the "lover";

12. Llull, *Libre d'amic e amat,* 241.
13. Llull, *Art de contemplació,* I, 4.

the mirror-image analogy; the notion of *sobria ebrietas* (sober intoxication), and others.[14] More bizarre phenomena may be encountered but they are mentioned charily.

Llull was in many ways an outsider and consequently looked upon with suspicion. This suspicion continued through the centuries, along with less vocal praise. Hegel, for example, remarked that Llull was incoherent and erratic. Recently, Lola Badia thought he was "hyperfantastic," his program a complete failure.[15] Not beyond self-flagellation, Llull often agreed with his critics, as seen in the *Disputatio Petri Clerici et Raymundi Phantasticam*. The negative appraisal of Llull reached its peak in the nineteenth century in the works of scholars such as Prantl and Littre.

There have also been many admirers. Aside from Leibniz, there is Mersenne, who suggested to Descartes that he consider the Art as a possible key to universal knowledge. Prominent thinkers such as Gassendi, Bruno, and Hobbes were considered to be "Llullists." Dame Frances Yates's view of Llullism can no longer be considered outrageous: it is not an unimportant outside issue in the history of Western civilization. Its influence over five centuries was incalculably great.[16]

14. Llull, *Libre d'amic e amat,* 43, 50, 100, 123, 283, 284, 364.

15. Lola Badia, "Estudi de phantastices de Ramon Llull," *EL,* vol. XXVI, no. 74, Fasc. 1 (1986): 15ff.

16. Dame Frances Yates, *Llull and Bruno: Collected Essays* (London: Routledge & Kegan Paul, 1982), pp. 114ff.

Llull was a failure in many ways. His short-range plans and elaborate projects went awry. His many visits to the papal court and the courts of kings were, on the whole, futile. His missionary efforts were heroic but ineffective: his missionary activity failed to convert Islam or renew Christianity. The Art was shunted aside and treated as an oddity. He did not become the "new Adam" of a society impregnated by grace. Yet, he was the precursor of symbolic logic and the computer. True, he was hindered by recurrent bouts of psychopathology that colored his vision and blunted his judgment. Outbursts were not rare. A good example is the crisis at Genoa, when the perils of the sea voyage he was about to embark on made him *tement per la sua pel.*[17] Nevertheless, he was able to break through his many disabilities to become a prodigious and innovative thinker and missionary.

He was a bizarre personality, and this is reflected in his thought and his writings. He was an extremely active man whose many disappointments did not deter him from his vision of a universal metamorphosis of spirit and the advent of a Christian republic. However, despite this, his importance to the political and social aspects of the age was negligible. His constant hectoring, his role as a gadfly, did not go unnoticed, nor, in time, unrewarded. What remains is his love of God and his aspiration for ultimate union with him.

17. Llull, *Vita coetánea,* 20-24.

Epilogue

WHAT does a fourth-century professor of rhetoric have to do with us? A man who spent most of his life in provincial Hippo Regius burdened with an explosive libido, a pious, domineering mother, and a weakness for the latest intellectual vogue, provided it was bizarre enough. Though the personality is commonplace, the man, Augustine, was not. He became a great man, the most luminous of the Latin Fathers, who gave the Roman Empire a worthy successor on a higher level, the *Civitas Dei,* the City of God. This replaced a secular society in which Christians were at best "resident aliens" and placed it beyond the realm of tangible things. Augustine's mind, prodded by grace, considered the problem of the individual soul in the *Confessiones,* society and history in *De Civitate Dei,* and the very highest reality in *De Trinitate,* not to mention other incursions into the complex web of cosmic reality. Although he did not succeed in restoring the Roman Empire (nor did he wish to), he did establish the foundations of a spiritual empire that would encompass earth, heaven, and hell.

Augustine became one of the creators of the New World that was aborning. He not only overawed the Middle Ages; he inaugurated a style of thought that resurfaced in the seventeenth century and entered philosophical thought, becoming a potent force from Descartes to contemporary phenomenology. His social-political thought remains at the heart of many of our most precious convictions, and his psychological insights remain of great value, even at certain points adumbrating the discoveries of Freud and modern psychology. Moreover, he stands at the very ground of both Catholic and Protestant theology and much of its social thought.

Augustine was able to break through the containing walls of his many interests and endeavors, shaking off the heavy weight of the terrestrial, aspiring to those heights of contemplation that he and Monica had barely touched at Ostia. Throughout his life Augustine pursued this light to its source and was able to pass beyond the realms of the spirit to finally arrive at that splendid, intense, unencumbered light that is the Trinitarian God.

Pope St. Gregory the Great was born some few hundred years after St. Augustine in an age during which Roman grandeur had greatly diminished and the Imperium had been displaced to the "new Rome" in the east: Constantinople. He was aristocratic, wealthy, and sickly; a man of hard views, unshakable loyalties, and a petulant temper. Called "the last of the great Romans," he exemplified the ancient Roman's discipline, tradition, worldview — and often his failings. Nevertheless, Gregory built up a church that was in serious danger of fragmentation so that it not only became a stronger church, but also developed into a spiritual power, dominating the West at least until the Reformation.

Gregory's works brought Augustine's lofty speculations down to the pragmatic level. In works such as the *Moralia in Job* and *Regula Pastoralis,* he structured Christian discipline and spirituality during the Middle Ages and, in a lesser way, even beyond. He was also influenced by Eastern Patristic mysticism. A century after Cassian, Gregory would begin with meditation on Scripture as the nourishment of prayer. The ultimate goal is "seeing God," and this can be initiated through progression in contemplation. Gregory's structuring of the church led to the reign of several "monastic popes." This trend in leadership, though positive, ultimately failed due to a strong clerical reaction. His exceptional practical expertise in ecclesiastic and economic matters was productive in the short term, and his gift for diplomacy, though often haphazard, was usually acute.

The "Romanitas" in Gregory's character produced a serious man, at times unbending, capable of severity, attached to the privileges of his station, never disposed to minimize its importance. Perhaps due to his poor health — intensified by serious bouts of gout — he could be-

come irascible and lash out indiscriminately. It was difficult for him to forgive an insult, and this could produce
an explosion, as it most likely did in the case of Justinian's
execution. But this should not dim the magnitude of his
goodwill, unfailing generosity, spiritual depth, and other
virtues that allowed him to deal with an undisciplined
clergy, the Lombards (and other barbarians), the exarch,
the emperor, and a host of others.

Though he had little patience with what H. L.
Mencken called "the elegant imbecility of the theolo-
gians," which he skewered with his acerbic humor, he was
kind and understanding to friends and acquaintances to
the point of excusing the oddities of a senile bishop. It is
easy to forget that Gregory wrote the *Homilies of Ezekiel,*
where his spirituality rises to the level of mysticism, and
that there are letters in his abundant epistolary that give
forth unmistakable sparks of light. A man of strong will,
the pontiff founded his own monastery and, after assuming the papacy, attempted to model life in the Lateran
Palace accordingly. He aspired to the life of prayerful
meditation, of silence, of contemplation, which is the
antechamber to that higher life which he would encounter on the other side of the present.

Anselm, separated by centuries from Augustine and
Gregory, is a man closer to the present. He came from a
family that, though it could be said to be financially com-
fortable, was, in the vernacular of the present day, dys-
functional. He himself was sensitive to a fault, something

of a "mama's boy," gifted with tremendous intellectual abilities and little practical expertise. Brought to Bec by Lanfranc (perhaps functioning as a substitute father, replacing the original, who was a difficult personality), he was initiated into the monastic life of prayer and regular observance, which he loved and would have pursued, had he his druthers, to the end of his life. However, when abbatial and prelatial responsibilities threw him into the world, Anselm was forced to cope with many practical problems, usually with little or no success. Nonetheless, he was adept in his personal relations, with monastic confreres, whom he favored, but also with others, including important churchmen and prominent laypersons.

Celebrated for his kindness and affability, Anselm would have been more fortunate if he had not been intransigent on issues that to him were matters of principle but to kings such as William Rufus and Henry I were of little or no importance. His diffidence concerning earthly things made the situation worse. But his apparent weaknesses were ribbed in iron — the iron of an intransigent monk who attempted to incorporate the Benedictine Rule into every facet of his life.

Above all, Anselm was a thinker. If God can be reached, it stands to reason that the search for God should take place through the faculty that is the most God-like: the human mind. In his major treatises, the *Monologion* and the *Proslogion,* Anselm ascends by logical steps to a nearness to God. Following Gregory's maxim that the prelate must be "the equal of everyone in compassion" yet "above everyone in contemplation," he goes as far as logical argument can go. Arguments stall, and the ascent is continued, but in a different manner. Having tasted the fruits of contemplation, the soul moves to a higher level in which reason is transcended and love — the love of God that is God — takes over and passes through the door of contemplation to the great, joyous unknown.

Ramon Llull, in spite of his eccentricities, religious and social aspirations, geometric figures, odd allusions, bizarre arguments, and surprising changes of pace, was able to play a role in the history of spirituality to which all else was subordinated. Active and contemplative at once, Llull was the first to speak of the "tree of the philosophy of love," which adumbrated a veritable avalanche of mystical literature commencing in thirteenth-century Spain.

His progression from his youthful folly to his neurotic episodes to his quest for sanctity adds a certain theatrical patina to his life. Still, from a life that was agitated and highly dramatic, he was able to inspire generations of spiritual writers to leave the everyday world and reach for the Ultimate Beauty and the Ultimate Truth.

It may be said that Augustine, Gregory, Anselm, and Ramon Llull were supreme escapists. They fled from their prisons — the cold and inflexible tentacles of the world — and were liberated. But even with the grace of God this was not achieved without great cost to them, and often to the church. The "wings of the dove" are often weighed down with lead. Each had his own life, his own temptations, his own fetid enclosure masquerading as Paradise regained, and each his own path of escape. Even though all had the same goal — union with the Trinitarian God — the paths they took were as different as their highly individual personalities.

Augustine was an enthusiast who radiated passion and zeal in whatever he engaged, whether it was sexual, social, intellectual, political, or religious. Once he accepted Catholicism and entered upon a career as a priest and, later, a bishop, he channeled his fervor into church affairs, theological debates, and intellectual probes that examined history, the spiritual life, and God. His intellect flowered, but eventually he realized that his speculations had an empty core and that he was obliged in conscience to laboriously detach himself from these impediments that kept him in thrall for so long a period. Ultimately Augustine escaped to God by denying his own prodigious intellect.

Compared to Augustine, Gregory pales intellectually — a tranquil radiance to a raging inferno. The dizzying transports of the African come down to earth as practical guides for Christian spirituality and maxims for the moral life. Gregory was above all a Roman conservative

— well-bred, aware of his status, and enamored of the monastic life that he attempted to establish wherever he lived. Sporadic flare-ups aside, Gregory led a disciplined life despite the many upsets, whether psychological or physical, natural or supernatural, to which he was regularly subjected. Surrounded on all sides, engaged in constant maneuvering, taking on the burdens of the papacy in addition to those of military commander and diplomat, among others, Gregory discovered a way to escape the encompassing tide. Following Augustine and the demands of the monastic life, he turned inward, leaving behind the incessant traffic of sensations, ideas, projects, wars, heresies, and other disturbances. Sinking into himself in absolute silence, he strove to encounter those eternal truths that underlie the "rules" which govern life. Though at first the soul may recoil when confronted with Divine Majesty, it is there that the experience of "uncircumscribed light" is enjoyed.

This vision neither restricts nor limits; rather, it expands the soul. In St. Benedict's vision, as related by Gregory in *Dialogues II,* the paradigmatic vision of the Early Middle Ages, it becomes manifest to someone who sees even a little of the Creator's Light that everything becomes smaller. The human soul is enlarged, the world constricted. The visionary rapt in God sees everything beneath him without difficulty. The soul is so expanded in God that it stands above the world.

Pope St. Gregory the Great was able to escape by

withdrawing from the storm outside, holding in check the exacerbations of his own quirky personality, and plunging into that inner silence that holds the Eternal Word. As pontiff, Gregory also had an external role, vis-à-vis the church, as protector. The *Legenda Aurea,* written at the end of the thirteenth century, reflects this role: "When Gregory was about to march over the bridge of Hadrian during the famous penitential procession, he saw an Angel on the top of the mighty mausoleum, the archangel Michael with a flaming sword." Pope Benedict XIV (1740-1758) fixed the legend by erecting a statue of St. Michael, which stands on the summit of the Castle of San Angelo. Like the ancient pope, he keeps watch over the Holy City.

Like Augustine, Anselm was a born thinker. But Anselm was also a logician, a man who deals with the vertebrae of thinking. The logician is, in a very loose sense, the puritan of philosophy. And this is exactly the case with Anselm, as the vast, multicolored world of Augustine has been reduced to bare essentials. Like Gregory, Anselm was a born monk. His style is more plain chant than polyphony, more an outline of a map on the wall of an ancient excavation than a superb renaissance *mapa mundi.* There seems to be an element of weakness in Anselm's character, possibly due to his simplicity. Undoubtedly, his familial difficulties contributed to his search for a paternal authority, which, in turn, coursed through Lanfranc and ended with God. This sensitivity produced a delicate, perhaps somewhat feminine (but hardy) sense of friendship, a friendship intensified by shared monastic ties.

Anselm was a dedicated — not to say enthusiastically zealous — monk, and as prior and abbot of Bec, he ruled with expertise. As archbishop, however, assaulted by a multitude of novel obligations, he was overburdened and often at a loss. His difficulties with kings led to consequent exiles; these added to the tumultuous character of his archbishopric. Often blind to the practical, he walked along dangerous paths, but did not lose his way.

In the shadow of Augustine, Anselm was gifted with a greater metaphysical insight than Gregory. He discarded the accidentals, the frills that impress and delight, and in a parsimonious fashion cut to the quick and followed the argument at hand to its conclusion. His major treatises take their point of departure from his *Prayers* and *Meditations* and the religious atmosphere remains, now melded with the argument he is considering. In the *Proslogion* the argument reaches the end of the line. Logic can go no further. At this point a spiritual motion takes the soul from joyous hope to the authentic joy that makes us full and more than full. Anselm escapes from the prison of his intellect and its logical framework and is welcomed into the highest of realms.

Ramon Llull was a troubling exception to any age, even his own, which proliferated in such bizarre personalities. He wore a number of different hats in his rapid, perhaps frenzied passage through the known and unknown world of his day. Two hundred of his works survive, the great majority preserved in Latin versions, though most were probably written in Catalan. He refused to abandon his Arabic mode of speech when prodded to do so by the Masters of the Sorbonne. He attempted several other unfashionable things, including trying to resurrect the old idea of the unity of the sciences, and to prove the existence of a new sense, which he called *affatus.*

Above all, Llull made a historic attempt to restore the luster of the divine attributes to a humanity which, living in a world that reflected them, lost its capacity to perceive their glory. The Art in its many manifestations, his encyclopedic interests and endless wanderings — the noise of his earthly existence — was muted by the divine silence to which he aspired.

This point illumines the difference between Llull and the other three mystics. They were obliged to still the claims of the external world so as to vault to the higher level of spirit in their approximation to God.

Llull, on the other hand, inspired by his Art, believed that the external world is a receptacle of the Divine and palpitates with it. Thus, his apprehension of God became direct and immediate. The obstacles which separate the human soul and the Divine were obviated, and for him the world became the theophany which, in reality, it is.

Postscript

W E LIVE today in a time of crisis. Humanity has waited expectantly for the demise of the West even before Nietzsche and Spengler broadcast it. This fear or expectation has been a constant companion. The marriage of Heaven and Hell has been consummated, and their progeny has been let loose upon the world. Population in the West has declined vertiginously, and blatantly anti-Western inhabitants live covertly within our borders. The enemy is no longer at the gates; he is also in the keep. And protection is at a minimum.

Tradition has decayed. Religion is despised or caricatured, with Roman Catholicism the villain of the piece, its bishops cruising on the clerical ship of fools. Education is in disrepair, culture perverted, and society dumbed down to a very low level. Sexuality of the most depraved and vulgar sort is imposed by custom and displayed in full color and sound. With the muting of social distinctions, civility and politeness have been discarded. The movements aspiring to political, social, and sexual equality have gone awry and given birth to monsters. The undesirables that a century ago would have filled our jails and sanatoriums have become by a strange metamorphosis today's equivalent of Lady Astor's "four hundred."

Society disintegrates. The leader-politicians of both parties inspire little or no confidence. The press is an instrument of propaganda, becoming progressively more destructive with each change in the presidential administration. The masses have been reduced to nodding acquaintance with the urges of the new orthodoxy of Political Correctness. The ancient perils to which civilization has always been highly vulnerable — war, pestilence, and natural catastrophe — are still with us, and with a vengeance.

It seems that we are boxed in, hexed, mesmerized — prisoners of a corrupt and corrupting society, abandoned by both man and God. Like Job, we are perched on a garbage heap while our sores fester and Harpy voices chatter. Overwhelmed by useless work and fractured dreams, we are being twisted into obscene caricatures of the society in which we live. We are in Hell, and Hell is both ourselves and others.

Difficult as it is, escape from this situation is possible. If we follow in the wake of our Saints, though hampered by our unsaintliness and lack of heroic qualities, we should turn inward while attempting to strengthen the outer ramparts of society. The traditions and customs that originally brought it into existence must be resuscitated. We are faced with a task that is both impressive and difficult: to escape from the commonplace that threatens to asphyxiate our souls together with whatever pitiful remnant of Western civilization still remains.

Wise old Plotinus believed that human life lay midway between gods and beasts and tilted toward both. Some became like gods and others like beasts — a sage observation. However, as Augustine indicated, Plotinus, because of his pride, turned aside from the only Being who could bring about his desired end of "happiness": Jesus Christ, the Word, the Lord.

Index of Names

117

Index of Names

Procopius, 12, 14

Recared, 14
Richard of St. Victor, 55
Robert of Normandy, 16, 80,
  83
Rufinus, 5
Russell, Bertrand, 1
Rutilius Claudius
  Namatianus, 11

Sabinianus, 45
Salvian, 25
Scotus Eriugena, 94
Seneca, 39
Silvia, 39
Socrates, 2
Solomon, 61
Southern, R. W., 66, 69, 82
Spengler, 113
Stephen, 26
Stephen II, 5
Straw, Carole, 47
Synan, Edward, 72

Tacitus, 3, 14
Tauler, Johannes, 85
Terence, 25
Tertullian, 25
Theocista, 54
Theodelinda, 46, 48

Theodore of Mopsuestia, 47
Theodoret of Cyrrhus, 47
Theodosia, 45, 46
Theodosius II, 6, 10
Thomas, 50
Totila, 45
Trajan, 50

Urban II, 16, 24, 65, 71, 76, 79,
  80

Valare du Bierzo, 61
Velleius, 14
Victorinus, Marius, 29
Vigilius, 48
Virgil, 39

Waldef, Earl, 81
Wilken, R. L., 43
William the Conqueror, 65,
  67, 68, 75, 77, 81
William of Malmesbury, 67
William Rufus, 16, 75, 80, 83,
  105
Wycliffe, 93

Xenophanes, 1

Yates, Dame Frances, 98

Zacharias, 5

Index of Subjects